When the Bough Breaks

When the Bough Breaks

Forever After the Death of a Son or Daughter

Judith R. Bernstein, Ph. D.

Andrews McMeel Publishing

Kansas City

www.andrewsmcmeel.com

07 08 RDH 16 15 14 13 12 11 10 9

A hardcover edition of this book was published in 1997 by Andrews McMeel Publishing.

Library of Congress Cataloging-in-Publication Data
Bernstein, Judith R.
When the bough breaks : forever after the death of a son or daughter / by Judith Bernstein
    p. cm.
Includes bibliographical references.
ISNB-13: 978-0-8362-5282-8
ISBN-10: 0-8362-5282-9
    1. Bereavement—Psychological aspects. 2. Grief. 3. Children—Death—Psychological aspects. 4. Death—Psychological aspects. I. Title.
BF575.G5B47   1996
155.9'37'085—dc20   96-33993
                                                            CIP

Dedication

This book is dedicated with love to the memory of our children.

Ross David Aaronson	7/16/53	1/20/89
Daniel Martin Abrams	3/23/65	12/30/88
Joseph Asterita	8/11/62	4/25/90
Todd Jeffrey Backofen	6/16/66	5/1/88
George Bain III	3/4/60	7/11/86
Steven Ross Bernstein	1/10/61	7/12/87
Cara Marie Bini	1/13/82	3/2/85
David Joseph Bradley	7/17/63	10/25/79
Robert Cannici	10/31/82	5/11/86
Danny Carcaterra	4/7/84	5/24/87
Jeffrey Louis Delia	10/16/73	8/11/82
Dawn Lynn DeMarco	8/27/70	5/12/89
William S. Edelman	4/9/52	2/1/89
Stanley Louis Ehrenberg	9/3/48	9/11/72
Robert H. Faller	11/17/76	2/15/90
Arnold Ira Feldman	10/10/54	3/7/73
Brooks Gilbert Friend	8/19/71	2/2/78

Stephen Paul Gant	3/9/56	1/7/88
Laura Susan Gifford	10/15/65	9/8/87
Christopher Goin	12/11/55	2/24/88
Edward J. "Ted" Gormley	4/12/63	7/7/85
Gregory John Gorzynski	10/3/82	9/17/86
Peter Joseph Heaney	10/28/61	5/5/85
Scott Merrill Helms	3/26/64	10/29/68
Robert John Jakubowski Jr.	10/28/66	10/31/87
Vanessa Michele Kehde	3/21/69	1/14/91
Judy Korin	12/8/59	3/15/82
William Leeds	12/7/66	9/1/87
Jill Lynn Leipsig	9/14/61	6/20/85
Douglas Levin	6/12/69	4/27/89
Melissa Deborah Levine	1/27/64	11/2/77
Steven Lipner	11/26/38	5/4/81
Susan Lipner	5/15/46	8/22/58
Robert E. Maitner Jr.	6/21/71	11/1/88
Bradley William Miller	4/27/68	8/26/87
Erin Mary Moorachanian	6/5/85	5/30/89
Robert Jason Morella	7/10/75	3/7/79
Sandy O'Connor	7/13/69	4/25/83
Stephen John Praisner	5/24/67	9/15/86
Paul Proios	3/5/61	2/11/89
Arthur Ravella III	10/10/77	12/7/86
Daniel Joseph Riedinger	9/4/82	9/20/86
Charles Conford Roth	9/16/71	4/17/83
Joseph Robert Roth	3/15/68	1/10/90
Gary Schneider	7/10/56	7/11/89
Debbie Schurmann	10/25/68	11/17/89
Max Raymond Smith	7/17/56	4/14/78
Michael Cahill Thomson	4/15/70	8/25/85
Gregory Mathew Williams	1/19/62	12/27/85
Christine Robin Wolfel	3/3/60	6/12/88

Contents

Acknowledgments

Except on occasions like this when I am called upon to bring the lens into sharp focus, I don't celebrate the act of breathing in and breathing out. I don't take the time to pay homage to the air that gives me life and tastes so sweet. Now is the time to do so, to pause and appreciate the extent to which my husband, Don, provides the atmosphere that allows me to flourish. His unconditional support and encouragement dispense the air I depend upon to sustain me. The arduous process of creating requires that sustenance as background, but his contribution to this book has been so much more than background. He has been a major contributor to the substance, from the interviewing, to the endless crunching of ideas, to the keen insights he invariably produced to lead me out of the dark corners in which I got stuck. I thank you, Don, for air, and warmth and light.

Robert McGrath, Ph.D., my beloved son-in-law, always available with advice and wisdom, generously lent his computer and technical expertise at whatever odd hours I ran into glitches. The title of this book is his inspiration. He is one of those giving people I feel fortunate to have in my life space.

Jennifer Goldberg Cole, graduate student and research assistant, conducted numerous interviews with sensitivity beyond her years. She spent hours in the library gathering data, books, and journal articles. Her help has been invaluable. Susan Borgaro read the manuscript in process. Her insightful comments helped reshape the flow and smooth out many rough edges.

Some children are gifted with sensitivity early in life. Such is the case with ten-year-old Alicia Mead Stirewalt, my son's godchild, who, listening to the adults wrestle with ideas for chapter titles, chimed in "Despite the Sadness." Way to go, Alicia!

Special thanks to Rosemary Ravella, a chapter leader at The Compassionate Friends and tireless supporter of bereaved parents. She introduced me to other chapter leaders, thereby making it possible for me to get this project off the ground.

My deepest gratitude is to the parents who let me into their hearts and traveled back through their anguish in order to illuminate the path for others who come after to this rugged road.

I am blessed to have two daughters, their husbands, and my three magnificent munchkins who provided the love and support that brought me back to life. You nourish me. You give me sunshine each day and hope for the future. Deborah and Robert, Wendy and Steven, Megan, Max, Brian, I cherish you.

Judith R. Bernstein

Introduction

My son, Steven, died on July 12, 1987. One day he was a healthy, gorgeous, bright, and loving twenty-five-year-old man at the gateway of his life. The next, he had a strange lump in his neck. Sixteen months later my husband and two daughters and I walked in a file to throw the ritual shovelful of earth into his grave.

No one could have prepared us for such a cataclysm. Initially our loss was colored by the year of horror, watching our son's struggle with cancer. We are both psychologists, surrounded by loving families and generous, knowledgeable friends. For the first months, we were wrapped in the warm blanket of caring friends and family. Later, we were lost. How are we to live with this for the rest of our lives? Will the crushing ache in my chest ever lessen? Can we ever return to our old selves, involved in the lives of our daughters, caring about our work, hobbies, friends, or the changing of the seasons?

How is it possible to get from this day to a time when you are once again able to enjoy the colors of a rainbow? And after the holocaust of grief has spent its wrath, can those colors ever be quite the same again? Seven years after the death of my son I was reading a professional journal article about grief and realized it discussed grief as if it were a finite period. Experts were saying that we should return to normal after six months or a year, two at most.

I asked myself how you ever get over this? What can be normal again after you've lost a son? I began reading more and more, ordering books and scores of journal articles from the library. I got so absorbed in it that the intensity of my quest surprised me.

A research project was taking shape in my mind. I wanted to interview other bereaved parents to see how they were surviving years and decades later. We know that we will never get over our grief and return to our old selves. But there is nothing written about how we evolve and what we become as a result of having our lives turned inside-out by the death of our children. To date, no study has been made of the ways in which catastrophe reshapes all that comes after.

I planned the project, decided what subjects I would explore, and set about gathering the information by interviewing parents whose children had died at least five years ago. Basically, I learned that most of us do get back on track after being derailed by the death of our children. However, it is not the track on which we had been traveling before our children died. Often we have an altered destination, new insights, new traveling companions, and new reasons for being on the trip at all.

We know that our grief will never end. We will mourn for our children every day for the rest of our lives. We will never return to normal. But we will live again. We will be able to enjoy the bittersweet colors of a sunset. We may be productive. Laughter is not out of the question. Life will be forever colored by what has happened. For every parent who loses a child, one life ended and another life is indelibly changed. This is the story of that change.

The Premise

Do you know the definition of a conservative? A conservative is a liberal who has gotten mugged. In that joke lies the premise of this book: Our attitudes toward life change dramatically following a trauma. We don't get over a trauma; we adapt our way of thinking and feeling about the world as a consequence.

Catherine M. Sanders, a noted researcher and author in the field of bereavement, wrote in her book *Grief: The Mourning After,* "Our culture has not been educated to acknowledge the length of time necessary to overcome a major loss. This lag of information adds to the burden on the bereaved because they themselves feel that they should have been 'back to normal' long before this." As time goes by, social supports diminish because "family and friends expect the bereaved to be over the grief in six months to a year rather than the three or four years that is generally required," Sanders continues. Even researchers who are working in the arena of bereavement put time limits such as three or four years for grief to be overcome.

Along with "overcome," the word "recovery" is often seen in association with grief. The premise of the current study is that grief, or any major trauma for that matter, is never overcome nor does recovery take place. The course of healing involves integrating that trauma, not overcoming it. There is a significant difference. To overcome suggests that you get past or get over the trauma and go on from where you left off. But that is not what happens. No one goes on from any major event in their lives without having that event change them psychologically in some way. The process of integration involves changes in the person's view of the world, in the way they relate to others, in their values, in spiritual feelings, and so forth. It's the difference between stepping over an obstacle and being rerouted by it.

Recovery: to return to normal; to win back, as health. Psychology is full of recoveries. People are "in recovery" from alcohol or drug abuse. People recover from childhood abuse or recover from major trauma or catastrophic illness, or so the theory goes. Recover, overcome—no, let's save those words for those situations from which we in fact do return to normal without alteration, as good as new. Like the flu. People get the flu, take aspirin, drink plenty of fluids, perhaps stay in bed for a brief period, and then recover. They return to normal, not changed in any perceptible way physically or mentally. But if we think recovery means return to normal, can we use the word to apply to conditions like drug addiction, like having been raped or abused, like losing your child? In order to lead a productive, drug-free life after a period of drug abuse, the last thing in the world the individual needs is to return to what was his version of normal. He needs a whole new way of looking at himself, of dealing with frustration, of relating to people; he needs new values, new attitudes. He should not be said to recover, but to undergo a metamorphosis, perhaps like a butterfly emerging from a chrysalis. That person needs to change, to find a way of sculpting the former life into a new lifestyle.

We cannot be said to recover, in the sense of returning to a former self, from any major trauma. Trauma as shattering and cataclysmic as losing a child, as rape or abuse, as addiction, as natural disaster, and so forth, leaves indelible imprints on our lives. We are not the same having traveled that road as we would have been had we been spared that journey. Events of bone-crunching intensity inevitably leave us different. The emotional journey people take to regain equilibrium, to be able once again to feel good and value life, to reform themselves so that their loss is somehow integrated into the fiber of their existence—that is the process of mourning. But if they are expected to recover by friends, family, experts, and ultimately by themselves, and they cannot do so, they wind up with additional self-doubt or worse.

This book offers an antidote—information—gleaned from interviews with parents whose children have died. This book will not talk of recovery. The premise of this book is that the word is a misnomer and creates a fictitious mind-set: that major loss is ultimately wrapped in a neat package and segregated from the rest of experience until it goes away. This, we know, does not happen without serious psychological consequences. Major loss needs not to be overcome but rather to be put into context. People don't recover; they adapt. They alter their values, attitudes, perceptions, relationships, and beliefs, with the result that they are substantially different from the people they once were.

Mourning, integration, adaptation. These are learning processes. Rape victims need to learn to live in a world in which rapists exist. They need to learn how to live with vulnerability, relearn how to trust, and so on and so on. The bereaved parent has to come to terms with a world in which it is possible for children to die, a world of different hopes and dreams, a world of muted sunsets. The victim never sees life through the same lens again. If you look at it that way, it becomes foolish to ask when victims of trauma should be over it. If we are to help and understand trauma victims, should we not ask instead where they are in the process of learning to live with what has happened? Where is that process in five, ten, thirty years? These are the questions I set out to ask.

The Study

My husband, Don, a professor of psychology at Fairleigh Dickinson University, had been studying the broader question of the long-term effects of post-traumatic stress disorder. We put our heads together in formulating the questions and methods to study the long-term effects of losing a child. We were joined by Don's graduate research fellow, Jennifer Goldberg Cole, and became a research team of three.

When we embarked on this study of what happens to people in the aftermath of the trauma of intense grief, we decided that the only way we would gain any knowledge of the moonscape of mourning was to ask those who had traveled to that barren, inhospitable wasteland.

Previous researchers like Ronald J. Knapp assured us, in his scholarly book *Beyond Endurance,* of bereaved parents' wish to talk.

> It was discovered that all parents eventually develop a primary and fundamental need to talk about this tragic experience and about what they can remember about their child. They develop an intense desire or need to reveal their sadness, to release their anger, to allay their guilt, and to have others understand their reactions. This is not only how they remember; it is also how they confront the reality of what has happened to them.

A major concern in asking people to participate in a study such as this is to respect each individual's right to privacy. We knew it would put people on the spot if we asked them directly to participate. After Steven died, I had gone to The Compassionate Friends (TCF), a self-help support group for bereaved parents and siblings, and I knew the leaders of the local chapter. I thought that asking for their help would be a good place to start. The leaders couldn't have been more helpful. They introduced me to chapter leaders in neighboring counties and states. Ultimately, five TCF chapters published our letter requesting parents to volunteer to be interviewed. The response was overwhelming. We had more volunteers than the three of us could interview. After six months and fifty face-to-face interviews, we asked the remaining parents who were waiting to be interviewed if they would give us a written interview instead. Again, the response was awe-inspiring.

Because neonatal death presents issues of its own, we asked for volunteers whose children were past the age of two. Since our study is about the long-term effects of losing a child, we set five years as a minimum amount of time since the loss and no upper limit.

As researchers, we know that people who volunteer for a study may differ in significant ways from those who don't. They're more likely to be outgoing, for one. We are aware that the New York/New Jersey metropolitan area is not representative of the world. Consequently, the parents in this study do not represent all bereaved parents. They do, however, cover a broad spectrum with respect to background and personality; they have lost children of varying ages; they are in good and bad marriages or none at all; they vary in education, social status, emotional health, religious affiliation, age, and cultural heritage. Some children died suddenly; some after protracted illness. Some died in accidents and some by their own hand. Thus, the interview group had a reasonably broad base.

To ensure confidentiality and protect the sensibilities of the subjects, we opted, though many gave us permission to use their names, to change names and identifying characteristics. We gave each interviewee an alias; so when you read someone's name in one chapter, he or she has the same name in another chapter.

In order to leave the greatest amount of latitude, we chose an open-ended interview format. We just told the parents that we were interested in how the death of their child colored their perspectives on life, their values, their marriages, their relationships with their other children, and with their friends. We did not have a list of questions or a structure but, rather, gave the parents free rein to explore the territory at will. Some lingered at length on one topic and others on a different topic with the result that we learned very different things from each parent. To ensure comfort and privacy, we conducted all interviews in the home of the parent. Each interview lasted about two hours and was tape recorded.

Each parent we interviewed told of an arduous journey, one more poignant than the next. I came home from each meeting filled with the tears, the warmth, and the wisdom of parents who had learned harder lessons than anyone should have to learn. I came away with profound admiration for the courage of ordinary people who never presumed to be courageous at all. I hope you will, too, after reading their stories.

The Accounting

- In all, we did fifty-five interviews, forty-three mothers and twelve fathers.
- The "children" who died ranged in age from three to forty-nine, with an average age of nineteen.
- The interview was an average of ten years after the death with a range from five years to thirty-seven years.
- The causes of death were:
  Sudden—thirty-eight
    Auto accident—fifteen
    Other accident—eleven
      Drug-abuse related—five
    Murder—one
    Suicide—five
    Illness—six
  Anticipated—twelve
    Cystic fibrosis—three
    Cancer—five

AIDS—two

Other illness—two

- The average current age of the parent was fifty-six with a range from thirty-six to seventy-nine.
- Forty-seven of the parents were married at the time of the death and thirty-nine remain married to the same person currently. Five of the parents were divorced at the time of death. One was single.
- Five of the parents lost only children.
- Two of the parents lost two children at widely spaced times.
- The range of income was from $12,000 to over $200,000 a year. The people at the lower end were retirees who had middle-class incomes during their working years. Everyone we interviewed owned their own home or apartment.
- Twenty-seven parents were Catholic; eight were Protestant; seventeen were Jewish; the rest unspecified.
- The families had an average of two other children at the time of the death. Nine families had children subsequent to their loss.
- The educational level varied, with seven having completed high school, sixteen having some technical training beyond high school, twenty-one having completed college, and eleven having graduate education.

(The numbers don't add up to the fifty-five interviews because there are many instances in which we interviewed both mother and father and, of course, didn't count the child twice.)

When All Is Said and Done

Years ago I was out of the country for several months. When I got to Customs at Kennedy Airport, the inspector smiled warmly and said, "Welcome Home!" The moment brought tears to my eyes. It was so good to be home. That is the same feeling I got in meeting the parents for these interviews, that it was so good to be home. That same sentiment is expressed by many of the parents; when they are with another bereaved parent they feel connected to a kindred spirit, someone who is on the same wavelength and speaks the same language; they feel at home. In our workaday world no one sees the aspect of us that is bereaved parent. As time progresses, we speak less and less frequently of the children we lost; yet those children are often no further from our hearts than our surviving children. When we meet other bereaved parents, we're home—with people who know that language and who understand the subtleties foreigners can never truly know. We can show each other pictures of the child we lost. Despite differences in age, religious beliefs, education, and all those other variables that usually define our social affiliations, there is a bond. The strength of that sense of connection surprised me. Many of the interviews ended with a spontaneous hug. Though we had known each other barely two hours, we knew each other better than most.

Ultimately, I think that need for bonding, the need to come home to a familiar place, is what motivated so many people to volunteer to be interviewed. Looking back, I now think that the need to bond with other bereaved parents was one of the factors that impelled me to begin this project. I learned a great deal from the parents I interviewed. I learned that I am not crazy when I see a young bearded man in the supermarket who looks just like Steven and I follow him up and down the aisles grateful for a moment with my son. I learned that I won't ever get over that feeling. I learned that I can live with that and still revel in the day. I learned that people have an inspiring level of generosity, a strength of character, a capacity to be nourishing to others when they themselves are depleted. I am indebted to the kindred spirits who accompanied me on this journey and taught me so much. I hope their voices teach and inspire you.

When the Bough Breaks

Part One

The Way Through
Mourning

Chapter One

Grief

LITTLE ELEGY

Withouten you
No rose can grow;
No leaf be green
If never seen
Your sweetest face;
No bird have grace
Or power to sing,
Or anything
Be kind, or fair,
And you nowhere.

—Elinor Wylie

The sun rises in the east. Winter inevitably yields to spring. The tides ebb and flow with comforting predictability. Seeds take root, push their greenery toward the sun, bloom, produce new seeds, wither, and die, all in orderly progression according to nature's plan. When an aged parent dies, though we may grieve deeply for the personal loss, the world is not turned upside down. Nature's plan, the predictability of the universe, remains intact. When a child dies, the very ground on which we depend for stability heaves and quakes and the rightness and orderliness of our existence are destroyed. Nothing in life prepares us; no coping skills were learned. Parents who lose children are thrown into chaos. The loss of a child is shattering, unique among losses.

There was a time when I thought that the word heartache meant profoundly sad. Then there were those many months after Steven was diagnosed and struggling through chemotherapy that I felt a crushing weight sitting over my heart and felt my chest constrained by steel bands that prevented me from taking a deep breath. I can remember going out to take a walk one day and feeling such an ache in my chest that I thought I was coming down with the flu. As I walked, tears began to wet my face and I started to sob but couldn't get enough air because of the tightness of those steel bands. I remember thinking as the spasm of grief subsided, "So that's what the word heartache means."

I didn't know it then, but that's what grief is, or in that case anticipatory grief, what happens when we're hit with the possibility of losing someone we love. It is physically painful, intense, overwhelming, confusing, and even frightening—frightening because it's so dark, so unknown, and so powerful a force.

Grief is an individual's subjective emotional response to loss. Mourning is the process of coping with grief over time. We will use the term "grief-work" to describe the tasks of mourning, the job of resolving the many predicaments brought about by grief.

Knowledge Is Power

Mourning is one of the developmental tasks in life for which we are singularly unprepared. We are unlikely to apply for a job for which we are totally untrained. Schooling and apprenticeships are required preparation for skilled work. No one would buy a widget that didn't come with instructions. But where do you find role models for mourning? Who rehearses for this drama?

A high percentage of parents we interviewed said they searched feverishly through books to try to find some instructions in how to go about this work of mourning. Books did help some. The parents needed to know what is normal, what to expect, how to face the dilemmas that confronted them daily within themselves, with their surviving children, with their spouses, and within the social context. Confusion compounded the grief, adding conflict and uncertainty.

I felt desperate. There was nobody who really understood how I felt. I was absentminded; I was confused; there was the insomnia until somebody gave me Xanax. I couldn't write anymore; I couldn't cook anymore; I couldn't do all the things I loved to do. I thought that I was physically ill and started going to doctors. I had my thyroid checked. I had all these strange feelings. I was angry at my daughter for some imagined reason. I had issues to deal with—my husband, my daughter, my in-laws, my parents; I was angry at all of them, for something. I felt that they needed me and I was annoyed that they needed me. I didn't have anything to give; I was vacant; I was empty. I wasn't sure that I was going to live.

Pauline

Many mourners report the experience of being in a maelstrom, having the sense of spinning out of control. They reach for lifelines. They read every book within grasp that might tell them that one day they may again find value in life. They read to reduce the feelings of isolation; they read to find order and predictability; they read to find hope. They are lost, frightened by the intensity of their emotions and the craziness of their thoughts. They are in turbulent, uncharted waters without a guide.

No one ever taught us how to mourn, how to deal with the intense emotions, the isolation, the chaotic thoughts, the dizzying ups and downs. Grief can only be described as a time of craziness when all the rules that govern life are suspended, when coping mechanisms that used to work no longer do, when the foundation and rhythm of your days are shattered into an unrecognizable crazy-quilt. Some people stop functioning; others hyperfunction as if nothing at all had happened. No one gets an instruction booklet about how to deal emotionally with the death of any loved one, let alone the death of one's child; it's too unthinkable.

Mourners desperately need to find order and predictability. Many seek counselors, therapists, clergy, friends. Some are helped and some find very uninformed advice, i.e., "You should be over this by now." That bad advice increases the sense of being crazy and out of control. It adds the burden of feeling they are mourning all wrong, that they are violating the customs of this alien land without knowing how to do it right and certainly not having the power to do it differently. Books and groups of other bereaved parents provide an anchor. It is reassuring to see that others are indeed experiencing the same violent, chaotic emotions. A few souls wander this barren desert together.

Self-appointed experts, professionals, clergy, and well-meaning friends and family are ready with solace, exhortations, and ultimately the admonition that it's time to "get on with your life," as if life could ever be the same. And yet, the experts have it down to a finite time period—a year, two tops, and then "get on with it," the business of living your life. Put the tragedy behind you. The expectation says that you've been derailed and now it's time to get back on track. When you're in the clutches of grief, it's easy to feel that you're abnormal, reacting too much or too little, or somehow doing it wrong. The uncertainty and confusion are compounded when friends and professionals suggest that there is a well-beaten path you should be following.

Professional and public attention to the processes of dying and bereavement have increased since the appearance of Elisabeth Kubler-Ross's book *On Death and Dying* in 1969. Her pioneering work served to propel inquiry into this vital arena of human experience. The past two decades have seen a proliferation of scientific study, new professional journals devoted specifically to the subject of death, books for the medical and mental health professions as well as for the public, media attention in the forms of newspaper and magazine articles as well as television programs that bring attention to the experience of grief. This expanding knowledge has the profound benefit of helping ease the journey for those traveling through the dark tunnel of mourning. Professionals, friends, and family are armed with information about how to be helpful. Mourners feel less alone, less crazy, knowing the steps others in their moccasins have tread.

> I read everything I could get my hands on. I wanted to know what psychological stages I would go through. I was trying to make some sense of what I was feeling. I read Judy Tatelbaum's *The Courage to Grieve* and I felt I had found someone who spoke my language.

I remember asking my neighbor, whose daughter was murdered three years before Hank's death, "How am I going to feel? How am I going to live?" She just stared at me blankly; I don't think I ever forgave her for that. She could have given me hope. I went to a priest in my parish; he mumbled something about prayer. I walked out of there and never spoke to the clergy about my pain again.

When it got close to the first anniversary, I saw something in the paper about The Compassionate Friends (TCF). I called Stephanie [the chapter leader] and asked her, "What do you do with the first anniversary?" I felt better after talking to Stephanie. After talking to her, I knew that there was someone else who knew what I felt. I felt for the first time that I might be okay.

Pauline

Information helps chart the course of mourning and is not only comforting and reassuring, but can promote healing and prevent prolonged emotional damage. This book will offer some of the lessons learned by fifty-five people who have sailed these uncharted waters.

Stages of Mourning

THE HOUR OF LEAD
This is the hour of lead
Remembered if outlived
As freezing persons
    recollect
The snow—
First chill, then stupor, then
The letting go.

—Emily Dickinson

Though many researchers in the area of bereavement discuss "stages" in the mourning process, all agree that these stages are

completely flexible and that there is no such thing as any orderly progression. Research has not found any evidence for the
existence of distinct stages of mourning. While there is no universal structure or time frame to mourning, there are many identifiable constellations of emotions and behaviors that occur with
some predictability. Basically, the progression of emotions follows from initial shock and numbness, through the acute grieving, to gradual adaptation and integration of the tragedy into
life. However, that progression is anything but orderly. People
may feel utterly anguished one week, numb the next, and
anguished again the next. Just when there appear to be a few
days of relief from the torment, something can trigger a relapse
into utter despair. Some people reported that the second year
was worse in some ways than the first. They said that after a year
the reality of the finality closed in. Sometimes an event would
precipitate a crisis and reactivate depressive feelings that had
abated. The word "stages" may be convenient, but keep in mind
that it is misleading. Not all mourners experience numbing;
some never appear to outside observers to grieve intensely;
there are no prescriptions.

Numbing

Veronica's ex-husband, never noted for his sensitivity, called her
one morning and told her without any preamble that their daughter was in the morgue in Arizona. He had just been notified by the
police that she had been killed in an automobile accident.
Veronica's first thought was that she probably shouldn't go to
work, although she didn't know what else to do. She called a
friend from work and told her she wouldn't be coming in that day.
Reasoning that people might be coming to the house, she got out
a mop and bucket and washed the kitchen floor.

When you cut your finger with a knife, your body reacts by
numbing. The pain is delayed. The psyche seems to react similarly.
When assaulted with news of a sudden death, many people appear
to go on automatic pilot. Some are immobilized and can't seem to
put one foot in front of the other without being directed. Others

are mobilized into action, immediately become efficient, anything to keep busy. At all costs, keep the demon at bay.

Immersing oneself in the predictable, familiar rhythms of funeral rituals provides an easy refuge. Order is imposed. People are present. While any complex planning or decision-making is impossible, following a well-worn path is simple enough. Many mourners go about making the expected arrangements, taking care that friends are greeted, and focusing their attention on meaningless details. After all, what else do you do when your child has died?

While a percentage of people keep busy and immerse themselves in minutia, another group of people become helpless and virtually nonreactive. They may sit and stare or take to their bed, not caring about eating or personal hygiene. This zombielike phase can last for weeks or longer and subsides gradually. There is no real pain, just a profound, immobilizing deadness. Along with the deadening of pain is an equally profound deadening of positive feeling. The ability to feel pleasure takes a long time to return. All activity takes on a robotlike quality. Life goes on by rote. Feed the children, walk the dog, take out the garbage, go to work. Ultimately there is no avoiding the pain of grief. The sadness, the longing, the anger, the guilt, creep in like a tide, slowly and inevitably, in different forms, at different times, and expressed differently for each.

Acute Mourning

Before people have had the chance to adapt and integrate trauma into their lives they experience a period of disorganization and emotional anguish. Mourners feel a loss of control over their destiny, a sense of spinning helplessly, not knowing how to get through each day. They walk around aimlessly. Day-to-day activities are done automatically but without purpose. Nothing has meaning. They grasp at straws, trying to get a handle on their chaotic emotions. This business of mourning is like landing alone on an alien planet where you don't know the customs or the language. Parents don't have a clue where to begin, what to do first, or how to get through the day.

All of the following symptoms are common and usual during this time of active grieving:

denying
yearning
pining
symptoms of shock
depression
numbness
anger
guilt
irritability
hyperactivity
disorganized behavior
difficulty making decisions
loss of interest in personal appearance or hygiene
obsessive preoccupation with events surrounding the loss
flashbacks
repetitive day and night dreams
seeking to be reunited through spiritual connection
sleep and eating disturbances
health problems
a sense of meaninglessness

These symptoms alternate in rapid succession. Some explanation or examples will help clarify.

Denying

"Denial is a shock absorber that helps us slowly absorb the truth," wrote Vamik Volkan in *Life After Loss*. Recall Veronica, to whom we referred earlier in this chapter, who set about washing the kitchen floor right after she was told of her daughter's death. That kind of reaction is both a numbing and a denial. The analogy of the shock absorber seems so right. The blow needs to be cushioned, wrapped in some busy-work. These temporary periods of denial are adaptive. They last only briefly.

Yearning

Theresa said that in the beginning she used to sit in Todd's room with his clothing in her lap. She loved the feel and smell of his clothes. She'd walk around his room, touching this, straightening that, drinking in his smell. She'd stare at his picture, filling her mind's eye with his presence. The yearning was profound. All her senses cried out for just one more sight or smell or touch of him.

Obsessive Preoccupation

Almost all the parents we interviewed related in the clearest detail the events surrounding the death. It's as if the tape of the event is indelibly etched on their souls and replays whenever something triggers it, even years and decades later.

> It was February 17. It was a very warm day for February. I remember, it was about 70 degrees. In the morning we had gone to the mall and come back. The big kids went outside to play and Ginny asked me if she could go. She kept begging to go out. I never let her out with the big kids if I wasn't going to be out. You see how quiet the street is. It was a Saturday and even quieter. It was about quarter after four and I let her go out with the kids. I must have checked on her a dozen times. She was out there playing when my sister drove up. I thought, "Ginny's gonna come in now. She'll want to stay in the house." My sister saw this car come screeching down the road and she screamed at him, "Slow down, you're going to hit somebody."
>
> The next thing I heard was the bang, it was so loud. I got to the front of the house and I screamed, "Where is she?" She was thrown not to the house next door but to the one next to that, I guess about 100 feet. My husband was giving her CPR and I was screaming. I ran in to call 911 and the police came. The policeman came and told my husband to drive the car. The policeman held her. I said, "She's not breathing." He said, "She's okay." We got to the hospital.

I still can remember, she was moving one of her arms and making a noise. That was the last noise she ever made.

Josie

Beth, whose daughter was killed in an automobile accident, said that she drove the police officer who found her daughter's body crazy with her phone calls. She needed to know every minute detail of the accident scene; what happened to the car; where her daughter's purse was; the condition of her child's body. She said she didn't know why all this minutia had significance for her, but she needed to hear the most trivial components. Most of the parents we interviewed told us in vivid detail of the hours and days surrounding the death. "It was very sunny. I remember because my sister was standing by the window closing the shade when the phone rang. . . ." And so it went, each small particular etched indelibly. These memories haunt mourners, replaying automatically and repeatedly.

Anger

Anger in the bereaved is many-faceted. It is common for parents to feel angry at the child for deserting them. The older parent who is dependent on the child, either emotionally or for actual support, may feel abandoned and angry. Parents will likely be angry with a child who died as a result of drug abuse or other high-risk behaviors. Imagine the anger if the child took his own life, willfully leaving the parents behind to grieve.

Anger is sometimes displaced onto others such as family members, doctors, hospital staff, and God, all of whom can be charged, directly or indirectly, with failing to protect the child. Displaced anger sometimes results in frivolous malpractice suits. Convoluted reasoning says that there must be someone to blame for a happening as untenable as the death of a child. The need to explain the inexplicable sometimes leads to blaming oneself or even blaming the deceased child. In either case, anger is directed at the target of the blame. Thus parents may experience guilt from self-blame or they may experience conflict as they experience both grief and anger.

Anger can be real and all too appropriate when there is direct blame involved. Anger at a drunk driver is real and deserved. Rage at a murderer who intentionally hurt and killed a child is unimaginable. Rage at the judicial system for all its lacks often consumes parents who are overlooked and insensitively treated.

Sherry and Matt's son was shot as he was walking on a street late at night. They said that the detective who was in charge of the case asked them, "Why was he in that neighborhood at that hour?" Each time the parents called the precinct for information, the police officers answered their questions with impatient and sarcastic responses. Not one of the officers or the detective in charge ever called the parents to keep them informed of the investigation. After years, the detective retired. The case remains open and unsolved. Sherry and Matt both have managed to move past their anger. Both sigh with resignation, knowing they will never know why their son was shot or by whom.

Irritability

The newly bereaved are impatient, have little frustration tolerance, jump out of their skins at sudden sounds, are generally keyed-up and overreactive because the adrenaline in their nervous systems is pumping. That excess adrenaline, like having too much caffeine, is a call to arms, creating restlessness, the need to move, keep busy. Along with the irritability often comes hyperactivity. There is a driving sense of having to keep all the ducks in a row, trying to keep control because life is really out of control. In addition to being an attempt to keep order and control, hyperactivity serves the second purpose of keeping the mourner busy enough so he can avoid the anguish that faces him if he slows down. In a way, the activity is a desperate search for what is missing, all the while knowing that it can't ever be found.

Cass's husband was out of town on a business trip when she was notified that their son was killed in an auto accident just a few blocks from home. She went to the hospital to take care of the necessary arrangements, made the phone calls, went to the funeral home and organized all those details, choosing the casket and deciding on services. She attended to each particular with businesslike proficiency. When her husband got home, Cass said he couldn't believe she had the strength to accomplish all she did. But it wasn't strength alone that allowed Cass to function with such efficiency; there was also an element of frenzy.

Flashbacks

Flashbacks come automatically, without warning or apparent triggers. They haunt the mourner. They fill the mind; they intrude, blocking out the present.

> For a very long time after, I played the nightmare movie over and over in my mind. I kept replaying that nightmare video up to the point of finding him lying there not moving. I had to make myself deliberately put it out of my mind because I knew it wasn't healthy for me to keep reliving it like that. It took hard work to banish it. It was many years before I'd let myself look at that tape again.
>
> *Loretta*

Health Problems

Stress-related health problems are common during mourning. "I worried a hole in my stomach," reported one father who developed ulcerative colitis during his daughter's illness. "I thought I was actually physically ill so I went to doctors constantly for maybe a year or so until I realized that the pains were not in my body," a grieving mother noted. "I had insomnia and was given tranquilizers." Headaches and periodontal disease come as a result of tooth grinding. An increase in cigarette smoking and alcohol consumption are often mentioned. Physical symptoms persist throughout the acute mourning. Five and more years past the death, few, if any, of our subjects report continued health problems that they attribute to their grief, with the notable exception of insomnia. Several say they had been sound sleepers before the death of their child but now wake frequently during the night and have trouble falling back to sleep.

Meaninglessness

What reason is there to get up in the morning after your child has died? It is the children who give meaning to life. They are the bedrock on which everything else is built. They are the hub around which life revolves. The person who spends fourteen hours a day at the office will often say he's doing it for the family, for their comfort and security. Even when there are surviving children, life seems to lose some of its purpose after the death of a child. Coming to terms with this vacuum of purpose is one of the important tasks of the grief-work. Parents often have to rediscover that meaning in their other children. They need to overcome the crushing lethargy and tell themselves that they must get lunches packed and underwear laundered. The gradual return of meaningfulness and the reinvestment of energies into life take considerable time. This reawakening of purpose marks the hazy transition from acute mourning to beginning adaptation.

A d a p t i n g

According to bereavement researcher Vamik Volkan:

> The course of our lives depends on our ability to make . . . breaks, to adapt to all losses, and to use change as a vehicle for growth. Losses not fully mourned—in other words, changes to which we cannot adapt—shadow our lives, sap our energy and impair our ability to connect. If we are unable to mourn, we stay in the thrall of old issues, dreams, and relationships, out of step with the present because we are still dancing to tunes from the past.
>
> If we are unable to let go when death demands it, we are often unable to hang on when life requires it.

Grief-work, like course-work, has a curriculum. There are tasks to be learned, emotions to be mended, and issues to be resolved. One of the early tasks of mourning is to undo the emotional bonds that make up the relationship with this child. What that means in practical terms is pretty complex. We shall look at some of the letting go, the new connections, and the new ways in which that empty place becomes filled.

Staying Connected and Letting Go
The following is a story of hanging on and letting go.

THE SHIRT IN THE CLOTHES HAMPER
The shirt was at the bottom of the dirty clothes hamper when he died. I found it there when I got to doing wash some time after the funeral. Life must go on in spite of what happens to us, and the wash was part of ordinary day-to-day life.

It was natural for the shirt to be there; I'd done his wash since he was born twenty-one years before. I stood and looked at it and decided to leave it there.

Year after year, wash after wash, I left it there. This was a symbol of normal life. My life wasn't normal anymore, and I left it there to sort of hang on to the past, I guess. It gave me comfort to see his shirt in the dirty clothes when my life was so extraordinary now.

One day in a fit of neatness, my daughter did the wash; and she washed the shirt. It must have been five years after her brother died. I felt a tiny surprise when I saw the shirt hanging clean in the closet, but I didn't feel sorrow or even disappointment. The time seemed to be right for the shirt to leave the dirty clothes hamper. A simple thing, but this was a symbol of progress of sorts.

I'm glad no one rushed me—I would have resented it. I was allowed this simple idiosyncrasy until it was natural to give it up. Left alone, I probably never would have removed the shirt, just left it there, never really knowing why; but when this happened, I knew I was getting better. Finally, I was letting go, and that was okay.

Fay Harden
TCF Newsletter

There are many facets to the task of letting go. It involves learning to walk past the cereal section in the supermarket and not pick up a box of his favorite, Cheerios. It means removing the fifth chair from around the kitchen table. It means appointing someone else to feed the dog. It means rearranging the way the Christmas stockings hang on the fireplace.

One of the hardest of the "letting go" tasks is facing the child's room. Whatever do you do with his clothes? How do you throw away or give away something he treasured? Deciding how to dispose of the child's belongings is a monumental undertaking. What do you choose to save for a keepsake?

Some families feel the need to attend to the room quickly, while others take years. We saw no uniformity in the way families dealt with the task of when to take on that necessary job. Some did it quickly, like an amputation; others set a date; for many the task of disposing of belongings was a gradual process that just happened over time.

> My husband kept telling me that we had to clean out Hank's room. I think he and the rest of my family were afraid I would keep it as a kind of shrine. I couldn't clean it out. But I set myself a date, that I would do it after a year. So I called my friend and told her I would need her help when the date came. She went out and bought new sheets and things for the bed. She came and we did it together. It felt good. I went through his things and I saw all his cards and I knew he loved me.
>
> *Pauline*

The driver of the speeding car that careened past Josie's house, throwing her daughter's body 100 feet, was never charged with any offense or even given a ticket. Josie mobilized all her inner resources to fight the prosecutor's office to try to right that wrong. She waged a single-handed battle, all to no avail. The grand jury found no fault with the driver. Letting go of that battle was a turning point in Josie's healing.

> It was a year and two weeks since she died and I got the final letter from the prosecutor's office. And I thought, "Well, I've

been through hell and there's nothing else I can do." I realized that Ginny was dead and nothing was going to bring her back. It was no longer important to pursue the driver. I did what I could and I lost. I don't have a regret that I didn't do all I could. I fought a good fight and then I had to move on.

Josie

The letting go is such a gradual and painful process. I have shirts of Steven's that I like to wear. The shirts have logos on them that are pleasant reminders; one is from a ski trip he greatly enjoyed, another is from his college fraternity. I imagine the essence of him still with these shirts. They keep me warm in winter as they did him. It's been a long time now and one of the shirts is in such tatters that I can no longer wear it. But I can't throw it away either. I compromised and tossed it in the rag bin, the home of all retired T-shirts in our house. I still enjoy the sight of it as I dust. I still enjoy taking it out of the dryer and returning it to the rag bin. Some things are just too hard to let go.

It's easy to see that letting go and staying connected are closely related. We keep the shirt in the hamper or in the rag bin until some time when it is okay to let it go. By that time we have found other connections that honor the child and keep the memory alive. Many parents stay linked to their child through the works they do and the memorials they establish. In Chapter 8 we look closely at the memorials parents have created that provide that vital link.

Connectedness! Finding ways to maintain attachment goes hand-in-hand with letting go as a primary grief-work lesson. Often, the manner of staying attached is also a manner of infusing meaning back to life. Research has shown that bereaved people who are able to find new meaning in life have a more rapid and healthier adaptation.

The parents we interviewed are living proof of the validity of those findings. Many, if not most, of our interviewees said that they agreed to be interviewed because they thought that telling others what they are going through might be helpful to the newly bereaved by making them feel less isolated and less frightened and giving them hope. Some of the people are still, after more than five years, intimately involved with TCF, as leaders, as newsletter editors, as resources when needed.

Six years after my son died, I started a bereavement group because none existed in our county. That's when I really started to heal. God led me to a place where I could help others. The group was a salvation.

Gretchen

Altruism seems to be an antidote for grief when the time is right. Letting go, maintaining connections, and finding meaningfulness are three early grief-work tasks. Thus, the curriculum for mourning includes: undoing emotional bonds, devising comforting ways to maintain bonds, finding meaningful activities that give life new purpose, banishing guilt, and allowing pleasure to revive. There are some signposts along the way. We will travel with some of the parents on the journey toward healing, through the discernable turning points and the more subtle, gradual evolutions that signal a coming to terms.

A Bend in the Road

Somewhere along the line, the load gets a little lighter and the sky a little brighter. The changes are so subtle that they go unnoticed at first. It is often only in retrospect that the turning points can be seen.

I was frantic for six months. I went to a psychologist who didn't know what to do with me. I went to a psychic. I was terrified that Kevin was alone. I went to TCF. I was working overtime because my ex-husband stopped paying child support immediately after Kevin died. I had to make up a lot of money. I went to the cemetery daily for weeks at a time.

At that time my pastor called and came to visit me. He said, "Your son is in the best place possible and you are going to be with him again." That knocked me out of the frenzy I was going through, just the assurance that I would see him again.

Regina

For Regina, the words of her pastor marked a discernible point at which the early frenzy began to subside. The beginnings of coming to terms with the death came in the form of hope. Finding within herself the comforting knowledge that she would see Kevin again gave Regina the courage to face the next day a little less frantic than the one before. That knowledge gave her permission to go on with her life.

The bereavement researcher and scholar Ronald J. Knapp gives a wonderful bit of advice to parents in his book *Beyond Endurance;* he provides a tow rope for parents to pull themselves back toward a meaningful life and a permission slip to abandon any guilt about returning to an enriching life:

> One thing you can actively do now to make the situation perhaps a "little more bearable" is to think of yourself as the living reincarnation of your deceased son or daughter. In a certain respect, after your child died you were really all that was left of your child's genetic endowment. Whatever your child had to pass on to the future can now be accomplished only by you acting in his or her behalf.
>
> Therefore, if you as a bereaved parent can think of yourself as an actual extension of your deceased son or daughter, this may help you to come to terms with the loss in a way that may not be as devastating. In many ways your son or daughter is still alive—alive in you, in your thoughts and memories of a life you have experienced together—and can influence the future only through your own behavior.
>
> Think of yourself as having an obligation not to allow your life to wither away. . . . Therefore, painful as this will be in the beginning, you should try to live the best life you are capable of. This is something you must reach for and work for. But, believe me, the price you pay will be well worth it in the end.

Knapp's sage advice provides a rationale to go on living when parents may feel like giving up; and, it provides the argument for living productively when they feel like copping-out. An important aspect of grief-work is for parents to find the courage to allow the shadows to dissipate. The darkness of grief is a connection to the deceased that is hard to relinquish. Enjoyment feels like a betrayal. After all, what kind of mother dances on her son's grave? How can your mind's eye hold the images of your child's casket and of a radiant sunset simultaneously? Knapp provides a rationale to do just that, to envision the dance and the sunset as tributes to your child.

Margot came upon a similar philosophy from a very different route.

After Marion died I threw myself into a frenzy of activity. I was working full time and decided to go back to school to finish my B.A. I went back to college and got my degree. I feel proud of that and I know Marion is very proud of me. I graduated almost when she would have. Now I'm looking to go back to get my master's. I'll tell you why all that came about. At one meeting of TCF, one of the women said that she could imagine meeting her son in heaven and him saying, "What did you do all these years since I died?" She said, "What will I tell him?"

I realized that I was going to go on living and that I have choices now. The choice is either that I do something positive to make Marion proud of me or how can I explain when I meet her that I've wasted my life?

For Margot, the conversation with her friend at TCF marked a discernible turning point in her healing. Had the conversation taken place a year earlier, it might well have fallen on deaf ears. Just as you can't teach a child to walk before his muscles are ready, you can't force the mending to proceed before the mourner is ready. The time of readiness is extremely variable. Some parents find meaning and purpose quite quickly. One of the mothers in our study, Gloria, whose adult son was killed in an automobile accident, found her daughter-in-law so distraught and crippled by her grief that she was unable to care for herself or the children. Gloria was galvanized into meaningful and life-affirming action taking care of her daughter-in-law and grandchildren. "The grandchildren brought life back into life," she said. Other parents remained in the deepest shadows much longer:

> For five or six years it wouldn't have mattered to me if I died. Life was a sentence. I didn't want to be needed or take care of anyone. Life was a burden. I don't know what happened, but life stopped being hard and a burden. Now things that made me sad make me happy, like songs and photos and remembrances.
>
> *Pauline*

> Last year on his birthday I was finally able to put his pictures up. It took me four years to do that.
>
> *Arlene*

Two years, four years, six years. It would seem that there ought to be some guidelines about a time frame that constitutes normal mourning. If there is, I surely didn't find any normal course through the grief-work. We saw instances in which segments of the grief-work got done at one time and other segments got stored away and rekindled years later.

Charles is a good example of deferred grief-work. Soon after Sheila died, Charles returned to work. As so many men do, he felt a strong responsibility to be both emotional and financial supporter of his wife and surviving children. Additionally, he is the kind of guy who doesn't wear his heart on his sleeve. He keeps his grief under wraps. Over the years his family healed. They created a life replete with warm family relationships and enriching and enjoyable activities. Charles is a stable, well-adjusted, reasonably contented man. Let him tell the rest of his story:

> My wife noted that I was acting angry a lot of the time and I went to see a therapist. I realized with his help that I was angry at the doctors for not curing Sheila; I was angry at myself for failing to protect her; I was angry at what she missed out on in life; I was angry that I was miss-

ing all the joy in watching her grow; I was angry that no one could comfort me; I was angry that my mother never comforted me; I was angry that my wife and I couldn't work on this together and were unable to comfort each other. After eighteen years we're still in different places. I don't know if we should be in the same place. We don't talk about it. That is a lot of anger that had to be worked through after keeping it blocked up inside for eighteen years.

When we talk about bends in the road and turning points, it is easy to see that we are hardly talking about one event or one time-frame. For Regina, one point came at six months; other points of healing came a little later, others a lot later. Charles lived productively for almost two decades before he found that there was yet another bend in the road he had not foreseen. Charles's story affirms the thesis of this book, that this business of grieving doesn't end, but takes a lifetime to navigate.

Residues of the grief-work show up decades later. Sometimes there is a key that opens Pandora's box. In Charles's case, perhaps the empty nest may have been a factor. A special event, maybe a wedding, moving from the home shared with the child, another death in the family, retirement, can all serve to resurrect unfinished pieces of the grief-work. What is most important to recognize is that the process of adapting to the loss remains ongoing and can crop up when least expected. The presence of bits of unfinished grief-work, however, does not necessarily encumber functioning in any major way. As Veronica said, "It's like going to a party with a toothache."

The lifting of the fog is such a gradual process that most people don't mark its lightening; they are simply aware one day that the sky is lighter.

Somewhere along the line, laughter happens spontaneously. And you stop and say, "Isn't that amazing! I did that!" It's a surprise.

Gloria

For me, there was a discernable turning point in which life became bearable and delight became possible. Pure enchantment came in a six-pound-one-ounce pink package three years after Steven died. My first grandchild and the two who followed were the fresh breezes that began to dissipate the darkest shadows.

Betty, similarly, could mark an event that forced a renewed investment in life:

> Two years later, Joyce got engaged and we decided that warranted a big party. That was a major turning point. Later, when Joyce got pregnant for the first time, that was a big moment.

Most of the time, coming back is hard work and takes determined, conscious effort. Parents say they have to "climb out of the well," scratching, clawing, backsliding, inching toward the light, one agonizing day at a time.

> Maybe a year or so after Jon's death, my job was in jeopardy. The company was becoming computerized and they began to lay off people. I went to a lecture on the new systems and about midway through, I saw this man speaking; I saw his mouth moving, but I realized I was not comprehending a thing. I felt like I could not learn anymore. My mind was gone from stress and grief. But I made it. I forced myself to listen. I decided to give it my all and I made it. It gave me great confidence, distracted me, and challenged me. It brought me back.
>
> *Arlene*

> About a year after, I said to my husband, "I want to travel to make new memories and to have something besides my grief." I booked a cruise.
>
> *Pauline*

Booking a cruise takes courage. Part of the grief in losing a child is knowing that your child was cheated of life's simple pleasures.

Many parents have the feeling that allowing pleasure is like stealing joy that rightfully belongs to their child. Secondly, being happy feels disloyal. Thirdly, relinquishing sadness means relinquishing a vital connection. Thus, giving up grief and permitting enjoyment constitutes a triple threat.

We've seen the harsh edges of grief begin to blur, the knifelike pain soften to a duller ache, and the seeds of a changed life begin to take root.

> A friend of mine who is also a bereaved mother told me soon after Kenneth died, "You're not going to believe this now, but there will come a day when this isn't the first thing you think of in the morning. One day you'll think of it and you'll look at the clock and it will be noon. You'll say, 'Hey! I got through the morning and I didn't think about Kenneth not being here.'" That helped! And, of course, the day came.
>
> *Loretta*

Signs of Healing and Adapting

These indications of healing are by no means exhaustive and one need not have each one to be on the right track. The manner and timing of healing vary with the individual. Even when healing is coming along well, and perhaps forever after, something will trigger a relapse and the parent will be back to square one, experiencing grief in all its intensity. However, these bouts—and they are bouts—become less frequent over time; they last a shorter period of time; the intensity diminishes.

- The amount of time spent in the clutches of grief diminishes.
- Time between bouts with grief lengthens.
- Sleep and eating habits resume a degree of normalcy.
- Irritability and disorganization subside.
- The ability to concentrate and make decisions returns.
- Flashbacks and preoccupation lessen in frequency and intensity.
- Physical health returns.

- Interest in social activities resumes selectively.
- Resumption of meaningful pursuits begins.
- The bonds of emotional attachment loosen as evidenced by:
  the ability to part with some belongings and
  the establishment of new connections with the deceased.
- Visits to the cemetery taper.
- Legal entanglements are brought to a close.
- Happy memories of the child return.

Complicated Mourning

People have a history, leaving some with a stronger foundation, some with a weaker foundation. Just as an earthquake leaves some buildings standing while others collapse in rubble, so the loss of a child interacts with prior mental and/or personality dispositions to produce different degrees and kinds of devastation. Mourners who have a history of mental illness, emotional disorder, or personality problems are at risk for having these old ghosts reawaken. The result may well be an exacerbation of their symptoms.

When the earthquake hits, buildings that are structurally unsound are likely to suffer the most devastating damage. People whose emotional stability is weakened have foundations that are more likely to give way under the stress of grief than people with more solid foundations. We will see the catastrophic effects on several parents whose grief is complicated by long-standing problems with:

- mental illness
- personality problems
- substance abuse problems

Mental Illness

Harriet suffers from the most profound self-hatred. "I am a poisonous person, monstrous. I am venom, a piece of shit," she avows in tears of shame and rage. Fourteen years after her car went out of control and struck another vehicle, throwing her ten-year-old daughter into the windshield, she beats her breast in anguished guilt. She recalls that she was daydreaming at the time and may not have been driving attentively enough. Was Harriet responsible for her daughter's death? How do we account for the extent of her self-hatred more than a decade later?

Compare Harriet with Boris, who dozed off in his poolside lounge one sultry summer day while his three-year-old played at his side. He awoke some ten minutes later to find his son floating facedown in the deep end of the pool. Was Boris responsible for his son's death? How is he able to live with his guilt? Eight years later Boris still blames himself, still feels a deep sense of remorse. But he does not feel "poisonous," nor does he hate his very being. He has gone on to live with the pain, to enjoy his surviving children, to lead a life that is satisfying, and to find pleasure and warmth with his family. What factors account for the difference in these two parents, each of whom must live with the knowledge that a moment of inattention resulted in the death of their child?

Harriet compulsively confesses her guilt in a litany that she has drilled into her consciousness. She has gone over and over her sins so many times in her mind that they emerge sounding rehearsed. "I'm such a sloppy driver. I didn't insist she put on her seat belt. That was the time when people were just becoming aware of the need for seat belts. My daughter learned about it in school. But I was distracted. My marriage was in trouble. I was obsessed with romantic fantasies about a man I was very attracted to. I wasn't paying attention." Raised in an observant Catholic family, Harriet's fantasies filled her with guilt. But none of this accounts for the depth or breadth of her protracted grief.

A glance into her background and family history reveals more salient explanations. Harriet reported that her brother was diagnosed with manic-depressive illness and that her grandmother had been hospitalized for many years with the same illness. Harriet too had emotional problems in late adolescence and was hospitalized for several months. In early adulthood she again lapsed into depression and received shock treatments. In fact, as she spoke of the early years of her marriage, it appeared that she had experienced numerous episodes of manic behavior. As a clinical psychologist, I doubt whether Harriet was a "sloppy driver" or that she was too immersed in her fantasies to pay attention to driving. It seems more likely that her manic-depressive illness produced the distractibility and inattention that led to the accident. And the devastating ongoing effects of that lifelong illness have interfered with her healing.

Boris, basically stable, with a positive self-image, solid marriage, devoted family, had both the internal and external resources to cope with the tragedy in a way that did not cripple him. A solid foundation served him well. The edifice of his life shook but withstood the emotional holocaust.

Personality Problems

Madelyn is a woman whose whole life centers around her children. She has few interests, few friends, doesn't drive, lacks confidence, and stays close to home rather than venture into a larger world that intimidates her. Even as the children grow independent, she continues to rationalize that she can't go out to work or pursue other interests because her children need her. In reality, she needs the children to remain dependent in order to give her a reason to keep close to home.

Madelyn's son became involved with drugs. His problems became a new and absorbing focus for her life, providing the perfect rationale for her to stay within the secure confines of her narrow world. When her son was in a rehabilitation center and he complained of the strict and restrictive treatment he was receiving there, she told him that he could come home if he didn't like it, thus sabotaging his treatment and providing herself with an invalid who needed her care. He came home without completing the treatment program, relapsed into drug abuse, and died soon thereafter from an accidental overdose.

Many years later, Madelyn remains depressed. Her life is empty and her guilt profound. Without the consuming purpose of caring for her sick son, she is emotionally destitute. Madelyn is an example of a person who functioned moderately effectively in the context of long-standing personality problems. She had become the co-dependent of a son who was dependent upon drugs. By protecting and coddling him, she became the "enabler," the one who makes it easier for the substance abuser to deny the abuse and consequently to continue in the abuse. The death of her child, whose disordered life gave her life meaning, left her feeling hollow.

Enid still grieves deeply eight years after the tragic accident that claimed her only son's life. As a divorced woman not yet thirty, she comes home from work at night, watches TV, spends weekends with her parents or siblings, and repeats the unsatisfying routine month after month. She told me that she longs for marriage, children, friends, and travel. The more she talked of her yearnings, the more she realized that these dreams were not beyond her grasp if only she would reach for them. She paused a long while in her recitation. "You know," she said, "I'm sitting here and letting life happen to me just as I always have. I got pregnant by accident. I got married to a man I didn't really love because I was pregnant. Nothing important in my life has been a decision or something that I planned. Everything just sort of happens to me. I'm miserable and depressed and doing nothing to make it any different." Enid came to a remarkable realization, that her characteristically passive way of approaching life had cost her dearly and was still taking a horrendous toll. I encouraged her to seek counseling so she could address these problems of long standing and perhaps find the courage to seek her dreams.

Substance Abuse Problems

I feel so isolated so much of the time. One day my girlfriend came over and found me on my bed drinking a scotch, anything to block out the isolation. She asked if I had a problem. I drink a lot of white wine. I like white wine. It's a wonderful way to relax. My kids will tell you that I drink much too much white wine. They worry about me. I knew I needed something since that first spring. I think I was more than the average social drinker before. I never worried about it, though. I don't really worry about it now. Maybe I need something awful to happen to me. I drink because—I wouldn't say it's a tranquilizer—it just relaxes me. I never took tranquilizer medication. It's a funny thing; I don't have a problem drinking white wine, but I would have a problem taking any mind-altering thing like Valium, or something like that.

Helen

People who have used tobacco, alcohol, or other drugs to cope with negative feelings are at risk for increased use and abuse of these substances when stress mounts. With increased use comes the genuine possibility of addiction as the amount of the drug need-ed to dull the pain escalates. As the amount of the drug increases, the severity of the reaction to withdrawal from the substance also increases, creating the cycle we call addiction.

Because of its widespread use and social acceptability, it is easy to forget that alcohol is a drug, no less addictive than the opium derivatives, cocaine and the like, or the stimulants, like speed. People who would refuse a prescription for an antianxiety med-ication such as Valium, as in the case above, because they think it is "mind-altering," think nothing of using the mind-numbing tox-icity of alcohol to ease their terror or dull their despair. Never mind the risk of drug dependence, possible addiction, and the ulti-mate destruction of brain cells; the use of alcohol and other drugs is a way to avoid facing a problem and thereby ensures perpetua-tion of the problem. The grief-work is not accomplished and the mourning becomes complicated by the effects of the drugs as well as the failure to address the loss and its attendant pain.

We have talked about some people whose mourning got stalled out because of problems that existed before their loss. Enid could not take the bull by the horns and direct her life because she'd never learned how to do that effectively in the past. Harriet lived her adult life with the guilt and self-blame that come with depres-sion. It is not surprising that an event as catastrophic as the death of her child should propel her back into her accustomed depres-sive style of thinking. It is not unusual for a wife who complains bitterly of a husband's excessive drinking to leave him when his drinking stops. The maladaptive lifestyle somehow fit and she simply is unable to cope with the new order. So it is with Madelyn, who suffered throughout the many years of her son's substance abuse only to find herself bereft of purpose in her life after his death. Mental or emotional problems that are reactivated by the stress of mourning interfere with the process of mourning. In such instances, professional help is needed.

Chapter Two

Factors That Shape Mourning

> And you would accept the seasons of your heart,
> even as you have always accepted the seasons
> that pass over your fields.
> And you would watch with serenity
> through the winters of your grief.
>
> —Kahlil Gibran, *The Prophet*

Rhoda stared into space, rendered nonfunctional. Her three-year-old was running a temperature on Thursday night with mild flu symptoms. Friday morning he seemed better but by mid-morning he was listless and feverish. The pediatrician told her to bring him directly to the office. She got there before the doctor arrived; the child had become worse so she went across the street to the emergency room of the community hospital. One hour later her son was dead of a massive infection in the tissue surrounding his heart. By that evening Rhoda was bedridden. She describes her functioning as "at the level of a two-year-old, if that." She all but stopped being who she was and remained unable to function for more than a week.

Donna learned that her daughter's car hit a utility pole; she had fallen asleep at the wheel. The police called to tell her of the accident and, at Donna's request, an officer drove her to the hospital. There she was told that her daughter had died instantly in the crash. Donna notified her former husband and began making arrangements for the funeral. She behaved in a highly efficient manner and greeted friends and relatives at the funeral as if she were the hostess at a party. Grief overtook her in the middle of the night; other than that no one could know that anything untoward had happened.

Mal's son died of a drug overdose at thirty-four years of age. Mal went through the prescribed rituals and ceremonies. For a long time he had vivid fantasies of finding and murdering the drug pushers who supplied his son with drugs. Otherwise, Mal's life continued as it had been. He went to work, attended fraternal meetings, and ministered to his wife who "is still having a hard time of it six years later."

Here we have three people reacting in very different ways to the sudden death of a child, an adult child in two cases and a young child in the other. How do we account for the differences? How long do grieving and mourning last and how does one define the end of mourning? What factors influence the course of mourning and shape its resolution?

Coping is the term we use to describe the way a person characteristically responds to life's strains. When we cope, we endure, alleviate, avoid, or surmount anxiety. Coping is a set of skills invoked to manage emotional distress.

When a child dies, people with even the most effective coping skills often don't know where to turn. They are thrown back on their overlearned, knee-jerk responses to trauma, which are performed automatically. That is to say, there is little thought; sometimes feelings are muted and the person may seem to be acting in a trancelike manner while engaging in highly efficient behavior.

Whether we cope well or badly, loudly or quietly, in isolation or leaning on others, stalled out or in overdrive is partly a function of personality, previous learning, and circumstance. We shall explore some of the factors that set the stage on which the drama of coping with the loss unfolds.

The loss of a child devastates the strong and the weak. The depth of despair, the acuity of the pain, and the sense of bewilderment are fairly universal feelings people describe. The differences in the course of mourning and the ability to rebound are influenced by a variety of factors:

- the personality of the individual
- the nature of the relationship with the child
- the general life circumstances
- social supports
- previous experience with loss

The next chapter will examine how the manner of death shapes the way we grieve.

Personality Factors

When we say, "he's aggressive," or "she's an overachiever," we're observing a personality characteristic so dominant that a person can be described this way. These enduring, reliably occurring characteristics—which we call personality—are both learned and biologically determined. (Later in the chapter we will highlight examples of each.) People usually remain true to their style, and can be counted on to behave pretty consistently from one situation to the next.

Certain personality characteristics seem destined to complicate response to trauma of any kind. People described as "nervous wrecks," "guilt-ridden," "up-tight," bottled-up," or "unstable," to name a few, are likely to have a different course of mourning from people who are usually described as "calm," "well adjusted," "adaptable," or "easygoing." We will examine some personality styles to see how personality impacts the way different people respond to the crisis of losing a child.

Proneness to Guilt and Self-Blame

The following case history of a composite of several interviewees I call Marcy illustrates a number of points that predispose a person to complicated mourning. Marcy's history, her personality characteristics, and her coping style interact to put her at risk when faced with trauma, especially the trauma of loss.

The child of an alcoholic mother, Marcy learned that her role in life was to care for others. She was continually blamed for "causing" her mother's drinking. People like Marcy are primed to think about what they did wrong, especially when it comes to loss of love or loss in relationships. Death is loss. Death of a child is the ultimate loss. Instead of mourning the loss, experiencing the pain, rearranging her existence and relationships over time, Marcy is stalled out in that old familiar place: "What did I do wrong? How could I have prevented it?" Marcy can't get past this. She continues to feel the loss—the guilt—the loss—the questions—the guilt—the loss. That is "complicated mourning" or "unresolved grief." It reflects the preexisting problems of the mourner; it does not cause them. Rather, it exaggerates them. Problems don't get solved; they get repeated ad nauseam in varying forms. The tempo may change but the melody remains the same.

We know that grief is a lonely experience. No two people grieve alike. Each individual feels isolated in his shroud of pain. Return to the example of Marcy, who was brought up in an alcoholic home. We know that such children live under a veil of secrecy, needing to hide the shameful reality of their family problem from their peers and often distorting their perceptions to hide the full extent of their feelings from themselves. For someone like Marcy, whose early training isolated her and taught her to bury her feelings, this aloneness is compounded. Furthermore, the isolation keeps her from checking the validity of her thoughts and assumptions with other people. If there is no one to question her assumptions of blame, she will continue to believe that she is truly blameworthy. She is more at risk for complicated bereavement than someone who comfortably expresses feelings and is able to ask for support.

Excessive Use of Denial

Continuing with the case of Marcy, we see that she was encumbered by a rigidly set coping style that predisposed her to get stuck in guilt and recrimination. Her need to hide the fact of her mother's alcoholism forced her to keep her feelings hidden even from herself, burdening her with yet another barrier to the resolution of mourning. Schooled in the art of denial, Marcy reverted to form when her daughter died. Her nineteen-year-old daughter was driving a narrow, winding road, missed her turn, skidded, and the car careened over the edge, killing her instantly. The accident took place on a Thursday. Marcy said her first reaction was that, since her surviving children were in college far from home, perhaps she didn't even have to tell them that their sister had been killed. After all, she reasoned, they saw their sister only on holidays. Her immediate response was to revert to the well-practiced defense of denial she had been using since childhood.

Recognizing the futility of that course of action, Marcy called her son at his college. She told him of his sister's death and that she would be cremated out-of-state where the accident occurred, so there would be no memorial service. Without a service, she told him, there was no need to come home and interrupt his semester. He should stay at school. She would mourn over the weekend and return to work on Monday. Ten years later, when I interviewed Marcy, her grief was still palpable. Denial of a problem doesn't make it go away.

Suppressing that volcano of emotions following her daughter's death took more energy than Marcy could muster. Despite her efforts at control, the grief would continually threaten to erupt. Following the lessons learned from childhood, she reckoned that an occasional glass of wine might help her sleep. Predictably, the occasional glass became a needed palliative. Now, she says, she drinks more than she should and her children have expressed their concern about her drinking. History put Marcy at risk for choosing this maladaptive form of coping. The drinking continues to mask the depression that should be treated professionally. It further complicates healing by introducing a host of new problems, social and emotional, which are attendant upon the disease of alcoholism.

Inhibition of Feelings

When a grieving parent throws himself or herself into a demanding new job, the work of grieving doesn't go away; it merely gets postponed. The likelihood is that the grief will return in a disguised form at some later date. Remember Charles from Chapter 1, who had a family to support and returned to work soon after the death of his daughter. Eighteen years later his wife begged him to seek professional counseling because he was uncharacteristically critical and short-tempered. When his co-workers echoed the sentiment, he was forced to take a good look at himself and saw the truth of the allegations. Early in the course of treatment he recognized the relation between his current out-of-proportion anger and unresolved feelings related to the death of his daughter. With competent treatment, he was able to acknowledge the depth of his grief for his child, and to complete the mourning he had short-circuited years before.

Perceived Control

People call upon a variety of coping styles. To understand different coping styles let's describe a minor stress. Picture yourself standing on a curb waiting to cross the street on a rainy day. A car passes, splashing your new coat with mud. How are you likely to respond? Would you tend to rail at the driver for carelessness and lack of consideration? Would you blame yourself for standing so close to the curb or for wearing your new coat in this bad weather? These two different responses reflect what psychologists call internal vs. external coping styles. One person blames others; the other person blames himself. Flexible people are able to use both styles as appropriate, sometimes accepting their own contribution to a problem, sometimes seeing that they were not to blame and letting themselves off the hook. Research has shown that people who assume responsibility for their actions to an appropriate and moderate degree are generally more stable and feel a greater sense of control over their destiny than people who tend to blame others as their predominant style.

People who are prone to blame others for their misfortunes are at greater risk for having emotional problems compound their grief and hinder their ability to move forward. There is a tendency among people with this style of thinking to feel powerless, out of control, and consequently depressed and angry. They may get stalled out in blaming, in legal action, and in railing against perceived wrongdoers at the expense of resolving their grief and going on to find a meaningful life. (A word of caution is warranted. Many people who have lost children can point to a very real wrongdoer such as a murderer or drunk driver. Those parents clearly do not fall into the category of people who blame others as a coping style.)

Though an internal defensive style allows one to feel more in control and consequently less victimized, even such a positive coping strategy can be used to excess and therefore lead to problems. People like Marcy use self-blame to excess and find it difficult to cut themselves any slack. Getting stuck in self-blame hinders the ability to move on. Extreme self-blame is like a life sentence without possibility of parole. Endless, painful guilt consumes the mourner.

In moderate measure, self-blame, guilt, blame of others, and anger are part and parcel of the condition of mourning. Regardless of the manner of the child's death, most parents feel some sense of guilt for failing to protect their offspring. But that guilt is understood as a feeling and not a reality and attenuates with time. Some degree of blame for others is often appropriate. In cases of murder, drunk driving, and the like, rage is warranted. Instances of insensitivity and questionable decision-making among members of the medical profession often incite anger. But the mourners who can leave the blaming at the wayside progress through the grief-work more smoothly than those who tote that burden on their backs.

Emotional Stability

One researcher gave a number of personality tests to a group of women who had lost a loved one two years previously. She found that those women who reported a low level of distress two years after a loss were found on the personality tests to be emotionally stable, mature, conscientious women. By comparison, women who said that after two years they remained highly distressed had personality styles that reflected low emotional stability and high levels of anxiety; these women had been apprehensive and worrying before their loss. Simply stated, people who are well adjusted before their loss adjust better afterward compared with people who start out with emotional problems.

Denise continues as a leader in The Compassionate Friends (TCF) seven years after the death of her son. She has been witness to the grieving and the healing of numerous families. She commented toward the end of our interview that she had had a relatively easier time in grieving for her son compared to some of the others in her group who appeared to have suffered longer and harder. She said, "I sometimes wonder if I had it too easy and maybe buried my feelings and that I'll be hit with something later when I least expect it." I told her I doubted it. Denise described herself during the interview as a reasonably confident, content, low-key person who had a good marriage, a wonderfully supportive extended family, many helpful friends, a measure of financial security, good health, and both surviving and subsequent children to whom she was devoted. It stands to reason that this healthy, stable woman would have greater ability to heal than another parent with fewer resources.

In contrast, Harriet remains depressed and guilt-ridden fourteen years after her daughter died. We met Harriet in Chapter 1 and saw how her history of depression interacted with her grief to create a pit too deep to climb out of. The backdrop of depression has left her too emotionally encumbered to work through the issues she needs to address regarding the loss of her daughter. Thus, her guilt remains out of proportion. Harriet was ill before her loss and made a problematic adjustment because of her illness.

In summary, healthy people make healthy adjustments and troubled people adjust in keeping with the nature of the problems they had prior to the loss.

The Relationship with the Child
Developmental Issues

Is it easier to lose a child of three or one of thirty? Is it harder to lose a child you adored or one who was endless trouble? There is no better or worse when it comes to losing a child; there is only "different." The tasks of mourning a child of three are different from those involved in mourning one of thirty because the nature of the relationship is different. Weaning from the relationship is different at each stage of life depending on daily interactions, emotional attachments, and the place that child occupied in your life.

I shall quote the wise insights of Therese A. Rando, writer and researcher in the area of bereavement, from her book *Parental Loss of a Child*.

There has been much discussion in the literature of the child's age at death as a determinant of parental grief. Evidence can be provided supporting claims that it is the loss of the young child, the loss of the adolescent child, or the loss of the adult child that is the most difficult bereavement for the parent to experience. Although researchers may argue about it, the clinical evidence suggests that the question is academic and meaningless to bereaved parents. No matter what the age of their child, parents have lost their hopes, dreams, expectations, fantasies, and wishes for that child. They have lost parts of themselves, each other, their family, and their future. This is often forgotten when the child who dies is at one end or the other of the age spectrum, that is, when the death is a miscarriage, a still-birth, or infant death, or the death of an adult child. There exists a curious social phenomenon of denying the significance of child loss unless it lies somewhere between these age points. When the child who dies is an infant, parents are told that they are lucky they did not have a longer time to become attached to it or are reminded that they can have other children. Parental bereavement is often overlooked entirely when the child who dies is an adult. The bereaved parents are usually pushed aside in favor of the spouse and children of the deceased adult. Nevertheless, no matter what the age of the deceased, the parents have still lost their "child" and the loss is just as unnatural as losing a school-age child.

It is true that the age of the child will define some of the specific issues that must be addressed in the parents' grief. This is because the parent-child relationship is colored by the particular developmentally related issues that prevail at a given stage in the child's life. For example, when a child dies during the tumultuous stage of adolescence, and has been actively involved in normal adolescent rebellion and conflict with his parents, his death may be relatively more difficult for the parents to resolve because of the normal ambivalence in the parent-child relationship at that time. This does not mean it is necessarily harder or easier to lose a child of one age as opposed to another; it is merely a different kind of pain.

Our informal research confirms what Rando noted, that neither the depth nor time of healing differs because of the age of the child or the age of the parent. The loss is equally devastating, the pain as acute and searing, regardless of the age at which the child dies. While the depth of grieving and the length of healing are not substantially different at different times of life, the form of the potholes in the road are different. Let us look at some of the developmentally related issues that Rando described as they are revealed in this group of parents.

When we talk about "developmentally related issues," we have to consider what meaning the child has for his parents at each stage. The very young child and his parents are bound together differently than an adult child and his parents. Parents' lives are more intertwined in the day-to-day activities of their young children, and therefore they have a difficult time adjusting to days that no longer include Timmy's car pools and Little League schedule. Very young children, by necessity, form the centerpiece of life. They absorb the lion's share of the attention of the primary caretaker. When that young child dies, the parent is out of a job that literally consumed each of her waking hours. In addition, young children are untainted. Our love for them is pure and unconditional, so that the loss strikes at the heart of our hopes and dreams.

A similar situation may exist for older parents who find the meaning of their lives again revolves around their children and grandchildren as the jobs and activities of their middle years wane in importance. Evelyn and Mal are in their seventies and retired. Their days are filled with friends, tennis, ski trips, and travel with an educational focus. To all outward appearances their lives are rich. But they feel empty. The anchor, the core of meaningfulness of their lives, had centered around visits with their adult son, the holidays and special occasions they spent together, and their frequent phone contacts. When their son died, the core of their lives was gone. They are left with the feeling that all the activities that they formerly enjoyed are now barren and hollow, without meaning. Almost seven years after the death of their son, both are still depressed and grieving actively.

> I don't recognize myself at times. I was always an active person, but now I'm running away. I can't handle having time on my hands. I have to have the calendar filled. I exhaust myself running. I blow up at little things, out of proportion. I'm aware that I'm ultrasensitive and that I sometimes hurt people. I have no purpose in life. What should my purpose in life be at this point? I don't enjoy anything to the extent I used to.
>
> *Evelyn*

As Chapter 5 explains, mothers whose lives revolve around the giving of care to their children appear to grieve more profoundly and differently from fathers who commit much of their time and focus to work. There is no study I know of to date that examines the path of healing in mothers who work full time outside the home compared with mothers who devote full time to homemaking. It is tempting to guess that people whose primary identity is "parent" and who don't have the emotional investment of pressing work demands have additional hurdles to surmount. The more ways in which people find meaning and fulfillment in life, the less crippling it is when one of those avenues is closed. That is why parents who lose only children lose not only the child but the entire aspect of their existence that was defined in the parent role.

In contrast to the unsullied adoration we have for a young child, our love for an adolescent can be tarnished with ambivalence. Parents are faced with the task of resolving the mixed feelings they had toward that child, the guilt that comes with remembering how very angry they were with her, how they nagged, how much of a tug-of-war took place each day. Parents of adolescents never come to see the fruit of their labors, how that child would have emerged when the struggle for independence was resolved.

One of the important tasks of the grief-work is finding new ways of investing the emotional energy that was devoted to the child. Younger parents have the option to have subsequent children, providing themselves with a new person in whom they can invest their love and devotion. That option doesn't exist for older parents, making it necessary for them to find meaningful commitment elsewhere.

Older parents have fewer options for ways to reinvest the emotional connection they had with their adult child. Helen is a case in point of an older person who seems stuck in the developmental period of former years when the role of parent defined the center of her world. Despite the fact that her son was grown, married, and living out-of-state, he still seemed to form the core of meaning and identity in her life just as he did when he was a child. Over the years, she failed to develop new sources of gratification. The weekly phone calls with her son, the holiday visits, gave her life direction and meaning to a greater degree than someone who has gone on to cultivate a variety of fulfilling involvements. Helen is grieving actively six years after the death of her adult son. She has no grandchildren. She has no meaningful projects that give her a sense of direction. When I asked her what purpose she found in life, she thought long and hard and finally said that that was a good question. In fact, she could think of no purpose in her life, though her life is filled almost obsessively, by her own description, with work, travel, sporting activities, friends. All the frenetic activity is designed to fill time so that she is not alone with her thoughts and her grief, but it does not constitute a reason to live.

Like the parent of a very young child who necessarily absorbs a great deal of time and energy, Helen remains "parent" first and foremost. Thus, the critical element in the manner of healing is not the age of the child but the extent to which the parent's identity is relegated to that single role. Helen's frantic activity is designed to avoid pain, but does not fill that void. Her husband, too, is left in the same morass. He says he no longer finds enjoyment in travel. They've traveled a fair amount and taking yet another trip is meaningless. They go out to dinner often, and another evening dining out is meaningless. Both describe squabbles they frequently have over "stupid little things." Neither knows what they are squabbling over since they truly care about one another. For both husband and wife, life is bereft of meaning.

Another burden older parents of married children face is that the focus of support is often on the spouse and children. The parents are often forgotten during the illness and after the death. They may be left out of decision-making about treatment or about funeral rituals. They may be needed to provide support for the primary mourners when they themselves are bereft.

Age also plays a role for the older parent who has come to the stage in life of being dependent on the child. We sometimes jokingly refer to our children as our old-age insurance. There is security in knowing that we will be looked after if we become unable to look after ourselves. The loss at that stage is both an emotional and a practical one.

For the older parent who loses a child with children of his own, there is concern for the continued relationship with the grandchildren. Daughters- and sons-in-law remarry. The new spouses may have mixed feelings about the involvement of another set of grandparents in their daily lives. Not every new spouse can be comfortable with the reminder of her predecessor. The threat of being cut off from close interaction with grandchildren presents a very real issue.

Different ages, different stages, different issues, the same pain.

Only Children

Enid is finding great difficulty resuming a life of quality following the death of her only son. Though she is a successful career woman who also enjoys her large and close family, she lost the aspect of her identity that was most important to her, that gave meaning and heart to her life.

Parents who lose an only child have a particularly difficult road ahead. They lose a major aspect that defines them. They may remain tinker, tailor, soldier, or spy; but they are no longer parent.

> I lost my identity. I had something I knew I was so good at. This is what I was meant to do. Being his mother was so fulfilling; I kept saying to myself, "This is perfect; no matter what happens in my financial life, everything else can go to hell, but I'm really good at this; this is enough for me." It was enough, very satisfying and extremely rewarding.
>
> When it was gone, it wasn't as if I could go back and say to the outside world, I'm still his mother. To the outside world, I'm a single woman with no children. It's hard to come to grips with. I wish there could be a stamp or a name for it, like widow or widower, some way I could identify to people when they say, "Do you have any children?" You could say I am ____! Bereaved is the only word I can come up with.
>
> I had in Brandon a real physical identifier. He was like an extension of me, a perfect accomplishment, and a focus in my life. When he was gone there was no focus. I couldn't go back and be the me I was before. I was still his mother. Emotionally, I am still his mother. I get a lot of comfort from the very fact of his existence. He was a wonderful little boy and that makes me very proud.
>
> I thought for years about a word for it. I need to tell people, I'm a ____. I want everyone to know I had this beautiful gift and it's gone now. I want everyone I see to know that I am in great pain. It would be easier if you lost a leg— then people could see it and say, "Oh! You lost a leg, how terrible." But when you lose a child, lose an only child, you've lost a part of yourself. I lost a bigger part of myself than a leg, the me that was important to me, and no one sees it.
>
> *Enid*

Just as alcoholics are said never to be cured, a parent is never "cured" of grief; that parent will never be a "former bereaved parent"; that parent will forevermore be a "recovering bereaved parent."

Life Circumstances

In addition to the personality and developmental factors that predispose the course and manner of mourning, the quality of life, in general, at the time of the death provides a context that can help or hinder the process. In the category of "life circumstances," we are including:

- marital stability
- co-existing stress factors
- support

Marital Stability

Chapters 5 and 6 discuss the effects of mourning on marriages, surviving children, and extended family. Here, we need to focus on the opposite—how marriage, children, and extended family affect the mourning. We know that grief takes different forms and proceeds at a different pace for each individual. Traditionally, in Western culture, men are more action-oriented and women more feeling-oriented, though these traditions are melting together in these more egalitarian times. It takes mature partners with a strong measure of self-confidence to be able to accept and allow for these differences under the extreme duress following the loss of a child. The mourning is made more difficult when these differences in mourning style threaten the marital relationship, adding an additional mountain to climb.

When her husband returned to work a week after their son's death and threw himself into business concerns, Patrice confessed that her immediate reaction was to feel that he certainly didn't love their child as deeply as she did or he would never be able to focus on work. She said she was initially angry at him both for what she perceived as his callousness and for his abandonment of her when she was immobilized. This mature woman noted that those feelings were transient. She rapidly recognized that his obsession with work was his style of coping; she guarded against her tendency to criticize his style because it was so at variance with hers. At a time when Patrice most needed togetherness, she had the wisdom to give her husband the right to be apart.

Allowing each other the space to mourn separately is one critical element that helps couples get through that first agonizing year. The demanding, criticizing, and blaming that take place in troubled relationships adds tons to the crushing weight of mourning. When each marital partner can reach to other friends, family, and outside supports and not make demands on a grieving mate, the marriage and the mourning are both relieved.

Respect is another element, along with space, that makes a vital difference. One marriage was dealt its fatal last straw when the husband insisted that they resume their golf lessons several months after the death of their son. The wife protested but was overruled by his logical argument that it was time they got on with their lives. Many years later she vividly recalled the mortification and guilt she felt playing golf when her son lay newly in his grave. She ultimately left her husband, but only after the several years it took her to regain the confidence his disrespect had eroded.

Sex is another arena for potential dissension, where a little respect goes a long way. It is the exception when both partners are ready to resume sexual intimacy at the same time. More typically, one will seek sex as a relief from the isolation and tension of pain before the other is able. Consideration for the timetable of one's partner enhances trust, allows the gap in intimacy to close gradually, and communicates respect. Failure of those necessary elements of space and respect within the marriage encumbers the mourning process.

Co-existing Stress Factors

Any stress in life is a call to action and depletes resources. Divorce, loss of employment, financial hardship, and poor health in ourselves or loved ones use our emotional resources. When more than one hardship occurs at a time, those resources are stretched thin. When there are too many stresses or too few resources something has to give. The person may just go "on hold," become numb and virtually nonfunctional. Multiple crises are associated with increased risk for impaired functioning in the long term. The boat is leaking more quickly than it can be bailed and threatens to sink.

At the time our son was fighting cancer, going through the chemotherapy and radiation, we needed every ounce of strength to support him and each other. But during that same agonizing year, Don's eighty-seven-year-old mother went into a precipitous decline, requiring more and more care. She wanted nothing more than to come to live with us as she recognized her inability to care for herself. We didn't know where to turn. We couldn't bring her to our home because she did not know Steven was sick and because we could not dilute the attention we were giving to him. Hiring round-the-clock nursing care for her in her own home was the best solution we could evolve, though it left us both feeling that we had abandoned a loving and kindly old woman when she most needed us. She outlived her grandson by several months, though we spared her that knowledge. Grieving as we were, we were less responsive to her needs than we would have liked.

People born in the thirties and forties are sometimes humorously referred to as the "Sandwich Generation" because we are the first generation in history caught between our dependent children and our dependent parents. In previous generations, children were emancipated at a younger age and parents died at a younger age. Don and I were caught in that bind worse than most and paid the price of feeling torn, feeling inadequate to meet the needs of two of the people we loved most in the world, feeling guilty that there was neither time nor emotional strength to do it all.

The Old World adage "It never rains but it pours" is apt in too many instances. The death of a child is never convenient. But when that tragedy occurs in a family already oppressed by health problems, extended family problems, financial problems, and job-related stresses, the resources available for coping rapidly become depleted.

Financial problems add stress upon stress. I developed an acquaintance with another mother whose son was undergoing chemotherapy at the same time as mine. She bemoaned the fact that she could not get to the hospital as often as she wished. The cost of gas, tolls, and parking was stretching her tight budget already thinned by medical bills. Obtaining and paying for child care for her other children was a constant problem. She said she always felt that there was too little of her to go around. I recall feeling grateful that at least I was free of having those added burdens. My counterpart had fewer resources and more demands upon them. The weight she had to bear was so much the heavier.

Support

Feeling isolated and alone is a basic characteristic of grief. We know that social support is a vital element in helping people to get through the grieving period. We shall address the issues of social support more thoroughly in Chapter 7. For now, suffice it to say that the presence of a backup team of caring family and friends is indispensable.

Often friends and family don't have a clue how to be of any help. Felicia was particularly lucky to have friends who went that extra mile.

> Would you believe that some of our friends went to the library to find out how to deal with us? They got together and realized they didn't know how to handle us; they didn't know what to say; they didn't know what to do to be helpful. They got out books on grief so they didn't feel so helpless. Now that's friendship! I don't know how I would have made it without them.

In the early days and weeks, the most helpful social support is in the form of being an accepting presence, ready to hear whatev-

er is said, ready to stay in the background when that is appropriate. Practical services are needed: cooking, child care, laundry,
cleaning, and generally keeping the family functioning.

> My sister didn't leave my side for a minute.
>
> *Belinda*

During the initial mourning when parents can focus on nothing but their pain, the other children need attention from outsiders
who have the strength and foresight to recognize their plight. That
help frees the mourners to do the work of mourning and relieves
them of the guilt they feel for being unable to do what they know
should be done.

Self-help support groups, professional counselors, and compassionate clergy prove to be invaluable sources of support to many.
They provide havens where bereaved parents find understanding,
acceptance, a place to unburden, and healing.

Support groups can serve the important function of offering
hope. These groups are places where parents can take off the mask
of social propriety, stop pretending to be fine, and be themselves.
The members who are years beyond their loss serve as role models for the newly bereaved. What many seek when they enter these
groups is to see what survivors look like. Brenda went to TCF two
weeks after the sudden death of her son, still in a daze.

> I wanted to see what the survivors looked like; how did
> they dress; how did they look; did they wear makeup; did
> they laugh; did they act normal? I just felt so bad. When I
> saw the survivors who looked normal, my first thought was
> that they didn't love their child like I loved mine. But they
> were alive. It gave me hope that the pain might ease.
>
> *Brenda*

In Chapter 7, we will take a more in-depth look at the advan-
tages and disadvantages of self-help support groups.

Parents who have backup coming from a variety of sources are
the stronger for that support.

Previous Loss Experience

Another important factor that influences the experience of mourning is a person's history of earlier losses. Although the loss of a child is unique among loss experiences, previous losses set the stage for our expectations and anticipations. People learn from their experiences. They learn how devastated they were previously and how they coped.

A young, dependent child who loses a parent, for example, is likely to experience that loss as a catastrophe. After all, a young child can't survive without a parent figure. He would literally die. A loss at such a vulnerable time would be life-threatening if the parent role were not immediately assumed by a substitute. At various times throughout development a major loss can be emotionally shattering if there is no one to provide the security, shelter, and emotional protection that are so vital to healthy development. In such instances, subsequent losses are more likely to be experienced with the same life-threatening intensity.

Author Barbara D. Rosof writes of Connie, a corporate executive, who functions capably at work and goes home each night and weekend to sit alone, immobilized in grief for her daughter, who died twelve years earlier. What accounts for such profound and long-lasting mourning? Why would a woman of such intelligence and professional resourcefulness stall out and continue to live in hermitlike isolation? Connie noted that her alcoholic father died when she was eight and her mother and stepfather died in an accident a few years later. "I got passed around among several relatives, none of whom wanted me," Connie said. Is it the traumatic loss at a tender age that made Connie vulnerable when a later loss occurred? Are the multiple losses what left the hole in her soul? Is the critical variable that her father was an alcoholic and the family dysfunctional?

Studies have shown that children, regardless of age, are able to survive a tragic loss, even multiple losses, if they are cherished and secure afterward. The important factor in determining how deep the scars will be is the quality of the child's life before and following the tragedy. Secure, healthy children who lead stable lives before and after a catastrophic loss will be far less at risk for future problems than a child with Connie's history of being shuttled among people who didn't love her or give her a sense of security.

In contrast, people who learn from previous experience with the loss of a loved one that they gradually come to live and laugh again have that knowledge to give them hope. They have the security that comes from remembering that they have survived those depths of despair. They have already devised strategies for coping and found ways to endure. Though losing a child is like no other loss, successful resolution of previous loss has some stabilizing effect.

We can see that each parent comes to the grief-work with a distinctive history and personality style that steers the course. Each parent has a one-of-a-kind relationship with the child that defines some of the issues that need to be resolved. Each parent lives in an environment that has both problems and supports that color the mourning. Since every parent carries different baggage, the journey must, of necessity, be unique to each individual.

Chapter Three

The Nature of the Death

I measure every grief I meet
  With analytic eyes;
I wonder if it weighs like mine,
  Or has an easier size.

I wonder if it hurts to live,
  Or if they have to try,
And whether, could they choose between,
  They would not rather die.

—Emily Dickinson

While the intensity of grief following the death of a child is equally profound regardless of the way in which the child died, the ability to adapt immediately following the death is substantially affected by the manner of death. We know that there is a great difference in the ability to cope depending on whether the death occurred suddenly or whether it was anticipated, for example, following an illness. We shall trace the course of mourning and the problems that each particular death presents.

Sudden Death

As Therese A. Rando noted in her book *Grieving:*

> While the grief is not greater in sudden death, the capacity to cope is diminished. Grievers are shocked and

stunned. . . . The loss is so disruptive that recovery almost always is complicated. This is because the adaptive capacities are so severely assaulted and the ability to cope is so critically diminished that functioning is seriously impaired. Grievers are overwhelmed. The difference with a death that is anticipated is that the period of anticipation placed the death in a context of events that were predictable and made sense.

In sudden, unexpected death, the parents drop into the pit of extreme despair. Shock, extreme confusion, and disorganization often occur. The world as they knew it disappears in a violent explosion. Their sense of control is assaulted. Life is no longer predictable or sensible. There was unfinished business, no time to say, "I love you."

Parents can't absorb this assault all at once. They need to take one step at a time. They need to take in the enormity in small stages and postpone emotions that are too overwhelming. It is helpful to let the reality seep in gradually at a pace that can be managed. Keeping things the way they used to be is one of the many forms this postponement takes. Remember Pauline from Chapter 1 who refused to change a thing about her son's room after his sudden death. It took a full year before she could contemplate facing that room and all her son's belongings. The anticipation of the first anniversary of her son's death terrified her. Somehow the date suggested finality, that she would have to take the next step toward acknowledging that he wasn't coming home. Knowing that the day was coming gave Pauline ample opportunity to mobilize the necessary emotional resources. In a sense, this period of time before the anniversary date was like the period of "anticipatory grief" that is experienced by parents whose child has a terminal illness. Her year of keeping the full acknowledgment at bay gave her the kind of breathing room that comes in cases of anticipated death.

Sudden death places added demands on the mourner. There is no time to prepare. There is no time to plan. There is no time to begin grieving or thinking about life without this child. But while the mourning following sudden death may be more complicated, often taking longer to integrate and sometimes following a more turbulent up and down course, research evidence suggests that long-term adaptation is not different from that of mourners following anticipated death.

M u r d e r

Murder is a special circumstance of sudden death that brings with it all the impediments inherent in sudden deaths and many more. Murder is one of the most devastating and painful of conditions for a family to endure. It is not only a sudden death that in itself tends to be paralyzing, it is also a violent death. According to Ronald J. Knapp, a specialist in the study of bereavement following murder:

> It presents the family with the very real problem of coming to terms with the fact that the child may have suffered before dying. This one aspect, perhaps more than any other, greatly complicates the family's ability to resolve its grief. Parents will often dwell on this aspect for months, unable to escape the thoughts or the horror that the thoughts conjure up. The anger and pain the parents experience over such an act tend to dominate their emotions for a very long time.

Not only is the death sudden and violent, it is also intentional. That additional fact produces a rage that boils inside. Parents become obsessed with legal resolution and revenge. The grief process is complicated by intrusions of police, lawyers, members of the criminal justice system, need for evidence, and the imposition of the media. Many families have to contend with public sympathy for perpetrators. After all, the perpetrator of such a crime may himself have been a victim of family, of society, of poverty, of abuse. Trial and sentencing (particularly plea bargaining) often raise the question, "Is that all my child's life was worth?" The insensitivity, slowness, and apparent injustice of the legal system add immensely to the parents' burden and keep them mired in their anguish beyond that of other grieving parents.

Suicide

Suicide is another special circumstance of sudden death that burdens the mourner with extra emotional baggage and encumbers the process of healing. Disillusionment, social stigma, guilt and anger, blame, and relief are characteristics that make mourning following suicide uniquely difficult.

Disillusionment

David E. Ness, a researcher in the field of bereavement, notes that the person who completes suicide puts a psychological skeleton in the survivor's closet and sentences the survivor to an endless pursuit of explanations. (The phrase "completes suicide" replaces "commits suicide" in order to avoid the stigma associated with one who "commits a crime.")

Rachel and Bruce knew their son to be an optimistic, involved, energetic, warm young man. He was an excellent student, a good athlete, had many friends, and an apparent zest for life. During a college break at home he told his parents that he had been depressed and was considering leaving college. They found a counselor who helped him through the immediate crisis and got him connected with professional help when he returned to school. No major alarms went off. The young man was experiencing some doubts, quite usual for his age. Just weeks later he hung himself in his college dormitory room. The questions raised by his suicide continue to plague his parents almost a decade later. Why? Was the happy-go-lucky young adult we knew an illusion? Who was this child we raised? They still feel a compelling need for answers. They are left empty-handed.

Social Stigma

A parent whose child completes suicide feels as though the suicide exposes him to the world as an unfit parent. Parents often feel that society blames and judges them for their children's problems. There are no identified cause-and-effect relationships between suicide and any specific pattern of parenting. Too many factors come into play in addition to styles of parenting to lay blame in that court. For every adolescent who completes suicide following the breakup of a romance, there are many more who go through that experience and rebound in healthy ways. The recipe for suicide contains many ingredients. Blaming parents is too simple an answer to a very complex question.

One effect of the social stigma is that these grieving parents sometimes fail to get the social support they so badly need. Members of the community may shy away not knowing what to say. Because suicide is unacceptable in this society, both the mourner and the caregivers are hampered in their communication. One of the main ingredients in the healing process after a loss is social support. Wrap the mourner in a blanket of family and community support and he or she is better able to mend. Take that support away, and the mending is all the more difficult.

Guilt and Anger

In the face of a child's suicide, the parents are "electively and publicly abandoned by a son or daughter who, in the minds of the parents, catastrophically showed that their love was not enough," according to Harriet S. Schiff, author of *Bereaved Parents.*

One critical feature that distinguishes the reactions to the suicide of a loved one is that the bereaved feel blameworthy. Self-reproach is common. The "if onlys" parade in endless torment: "if only I had paid more attention"; "if only I hadn't gone to work"; "I should have indulged him more"; "I should have indulged him less." Contradicting voices echo through the soul. "What did I do wrong?" "What could I have done differently?" While parents whose child died in a "preventable" accident harbor guilt for failing to protect the child, their lapse was a momentary one. In contrast, the child who completes suicide can too readily be interpreted as making a blanket indictment of the parents as failures. There is no evidence, however, that even abused children are more likely to take their own lives. But while no evidence exists to point a finger at parents, parents continue to point the finger of blame at themselves.

Guilt is often a long-lasting burden carried by parents whose children take their own lives. Self-reproach is prominent in these parents regardless of their personality styles. They often blame themselves for not recognizing the depth of their child's despair and taking action. They typically ask themselves over and over how they were wanting as parents. It is the manner of death and not the personality of the mourner, in this case, that predisposes these parents to a more difficult course through mourning.

Anger at the child is common. First there is the anger that the child chose to leave you. There is the anger that your lives were thrown into chaos. There is the anger that you were deprived of their company, their children, their futures, by a willful act.

Blame

When I asked Theda to tell me how her son died, she replied, "I need to tell you something that happened when he was two." She proceeded to recount an incident that highlighted her husband's harsh, rejecting treatment of her son. She went on to explain how this cold, withdrawn, neglectful man continued throughout her son's life to diminish the boy and rob him of confidence. While trying to convince herself of her husband's responsibility for her son's suicide, she was not able to spare herself. Theda mourned her cowardice and timidity in allowing the situation to persist through two decades and in failing to protect her son from this toxic man. Blame is a pernicious thing. Ultimately this marriage ended. But Theda continues to shoulder her burden of self-blame.

Ann Smolin and John Guinan, leaders of suicide survivor support groups, noted, however, that open expression of blame can have positive results. The context of a support group, especially one with a leader who can provide limits and structure, can be a protected environment in which the angriest feelings can be expressed safely. These therapists conclude that, "Couples who are most openly angry with each other after the suicide of their children often come to the most workable reconciliations." They reason that once the couple has heard each other's accusations, they no longer need to be afraid of what the other is thinking. The worst has been said. From that point, further communication and forgiving can ensue. The value of open communication is under-scored.

Relief

Children don't complete suicide in a vacuum. Often there was a lengthy period of serious problems that preceded the act. There may have been school problems, severe emotional problems, hos-pitalizations, treatment, soul-searching, and long and arduous attempts to help the troubled youngster. Anguished middle-of-the-night phone calls from a depressed young adult exact an enor-mous toll on caring parents. The parents so often feel helpless. This troubled offspring consumes their energies, takes them from their other children, and deprives them of peace and order. Much to their own shock and horror, some parents find themselves experi-encing relief that they no longer need to live in fear of what the next phone call may bring.

Drug Abuse or Other Antisocial Acts

Pamela sat in the support group circle slumped in her seat, the pic-ture of defeat. Her speech was slow and soft.

> My son was into drinking and drugs. He stole and was in jail once. He was in and out of rehabilitation centers, but it didn't help. When he died, it seemed like everybody just said, "Good riddance to bad rubbish" and shrugged it off. But he was my son!

Is Pamela's suffering less than the parent of the ideal, high-achieving son? Hardly! Her suffering is compounded by the sor-row for her son's beleaguered life and for the joy he didn't have for himself or give to her. Her ability to come to terms is bur-dened by the fact that too few are saying, "What a tragedy," and giving her the sympathy she deserves. Parents who grieve for children who lived lives at variance with social norms are too often isolated and punished. They join parents of children who completed suicide and adult children who had AIDS in being the pariahs, deprived of their rightful share of compassion.

Anticipated Death

The sunny Sunday morning my son died I didn't cry. His breathing had gotten shallower and shallower until I couldn't hear it any longer. I walked outside his room and told a nurse I thought he might not be breathing. She called a doctor who came in, listened, nodded slightly, whispered, "I'm sorry," and quietly left.

No strangers to death and grief, the oncology staff of the hospital were thoroughly respectful of our needs. They gave us privacy; they gave us time; they made available a room and a phone. After a while they told us what needed to be done and guided us through the rituals.

Judith

Death that comes after a long illness is a quieter experience than the utter turmoil after sudden death—no less painful, just less turbulent. In sudden death, the family is plunged immediately into the abyss of despair. A very different route is traveled when death is anticipated.

I'll never forget the moment we received the news that the tumor was malignant. My heart was pounding so loudly in my ears that I could hardly hear. I couldn't catch my breath and kept gasping for air. I started to shake all over. I felt like the world was coming to an end.

Judith

For parents whose children are diagnosed with cancer or other life-threatening disease, the pit of despair and anguish comes more often with the diagnosis than with the death. Unlike parents whose children die suddenly, these parents often are given a ray of hope, a period of time to absorb the enormity of what is happening to their lives. Hope comes in the form of treatment plans. Despair is set aside as the family mobilizes to begin the treatments. A new order is established as the therapy regimen proceeds and attention is focused on getting well and achieving a remission or a cure. Life resumes a parody of normalcy and despair is temporarily held at arm's length.

But the reality of the possibility of losing this child is never far from consciousness. These parents have some chance to prepare. Throughout the treatment and throughout the hope grieving continues. This "anticipatory grief," as it is called, is what changes the course of mourning after death. Part of the grief-work has been done.

From the pit of despair following diagnosis, through the lightening during treatment, a new kind of despair returns as death approaches. It is a duller, pervasive ache, different from the sharp and piercing pain that preceded. It is during this agonizing time that more of the vital work of grief gets done. The intensity of the caretaking often provides an expiation of guilt. You have a sense that you have done all that you could do. You have had a chance to say what needed to be said, to give what comfort needed to be given, to pour out love and caring and commitment.

> We didn't want our son to be alone any time he was in the hospital. We made sure one or more of us was there day and night. The hospital staff made us as comfortable as possible. We took turns sleeping in a lounge chair by his side each night. It had to be done. One of us was beside him every moment for that whole six-week period. The morphine made him a little high and there were times he told us about his adventures that had us all in stitches. Other times he talked about the hopes and dreams he had for his life. We listened, and talked, and laughed, and cried. It was intense beyond belief. I don't know how we got through. But, in the long run, it helped. We knew we were there for him and had no guilt afterward.
>
> *Judith*

The time of dying is exhausting in every way. When death comes, often there is a small sense of relief. That fleeting feeling passes and the long bout with grief begins. But since a measure of the grief-work has already been going on for some time, the arduous journey can be somewhat shorter and less stormy than it is when death is sudden.

AIDS

Do you feel the same surge of compassion for a parent whose gay son died from AIDS as you do for one whose son died from leukemia? What marks the differences in those feelings? What are you telling yourself about each?

Tragically, AIDS carries with it a social stigma. The parents of the AIDS victim are no different from the public at large and sometimes are burdened doubly, by having a sick child and by having to do battle with those prejudices even within themselves.

Don and I interviewed a couple in different rooms of their home at the same time. When I asked the mother the cause of death, she replied, "AIDS." She then asked if my husband would be asking her husband the same question. I said I thought that was likely. She remarked that her husband had difficulty acknowledging the cause of death publicly and frequently resorted to the half-truth of saying that their son died of pneumonia. He was, she noted, shamed by the association between AIDS and homosexuality, though their son was not gay. In fact, he said his son died of Pneumocystis pneumonia, which clearly spells AIDS but gets around the need to say the dreaded word. This bereaved father's grief was compounded by having to work through attitudes his culture had instilled. As if losing a son was not bad enough, he was additionally weighted by social stigma.

In another instance, the stigma surrounding AIDS infected the priest who had known the family a long time. When the priest came to the hospital to visit, as his responsibilities required, he stood outside the room, refusing to enter for fear of contagion. The family suffered the loss of much-needed support; it suffered the outrage of being shunned by someone who should have known better, all the while contending with the gradual weakening of their child.

The family who lives with the diagnosis of AIDS lives each day with its ear tuned to the drumbeats of experimental medications, of this new therapy, of that rumored treatment, of hope for prolonged life in the forms of vitamins, dietary regimens, exercise, or meditation. It lives with prejudice, fear, and segregation.

Like leukemia, AIDS is a hideous disease that saps its victims by slow and painful degree. Parents endure a roller-coaster of anguish and hope, often for years, and ultimately watch a process of degeneration. The grief of these parents is compounded by the years of suffering preceding the death, by the sometimes painful manner of dying, and by misunderstanding.

A self-help support and activist group, Mother's Voices, offers help to parents whose children are living with or have died from AIDS.

From this brief exploration of the nature of grief and the forces that shape the grief-work, we go on to see how parents begin to adapt. We will hear them tell how they changed within themselves and in all the relationships they value.

Part Two

The Rest of Our Lives

Chapter Four

Despite the Sadness:
Altered Perspectives

I dreaded that first robin so,
But he is mastered now,
And I'm accustomed to him grown,—
He hurts a little, though.

—Emily Dickinson

Steven was spring skiing in March of 1986. When he came home he said he had had a wonderful time in the perfect conditions but that he had felt tired and couldn't keep up his usual dawn to dusk pace. He suspected he had a bug and made an appointment with our internist, Marc. I wasn't alarmed; bugs aren't serious in this day and age. When the doctor ordered an X ray, my thought was that he was ruling out pneumonia and I still felt little alarm. I had a date to meet my daughter at her college that evening to go out to dinner with her. When we were waiting for our meal to be served, I decided to call home to find out the results of the X ray; there was no answer. A couple of hours later I got home to find my husband and Steven sitting at the kitchen table looking ashen and stunned. My husband said quietly, "Marc thinks Steven has Hodgkin's." (It turned out that Steven had a non-Hodgkin's lymphoma, a less responsive cancer cell than Hodgkin's, so the news was even more catastrophic than we knew then.) The ground opened at that moment and swallowed me. Nothing in life has ever been the same since.

Years later I walked along a section of the San Andreas Fault on an idyllic summer afternoon. The forest radiated calm. Birds chirped and squirrels scampered, completing the portrait of peace and harmony. But over there a stream bed was suddenly interrupted and its interlocking puzzle piece lay several feet to the west and slightly higher. Here a tree stood, twisted, but apparently strong and healthy. The fault remained as evidence that a cataclysm rent the land in two some long time past. The analogy with life following the pronouncement of "lymphoma" was striking. No human effort could put the puzzle back to its original; the landscape was irrevocably altered. Yet ultimately, a much altered form of peace and harmony returned and life in its new incarnation continued.

In Chapters 1, 2, and 3 we reviewed the dark shadows of grief and the factors that shape its features. The shadows do begin to lighten ever so slowly, almost imperceptibly, over time; but the landscape has changed. The message of this book is that parents do not "return to normal" after losing a child. Rather, the ordeal, like the earthquake, changes the terrain of our lives in subtle but substantial ways. Such is the nature of grief. It leaves the mourner much like the wedding guest in Coleridge's *The Rime of the Ancient Mariner*, "A sadder and a wiser man, he rose the morrow morn."

As Ida M. Martinson noted in an article she wrote for a professional journal:

> ... bereaved parents do not "recover" in the sense of returning to who they were before the death. Instead, they appear to change as they integrate the loss into their lives.

When we asked parents to compare themselves before and after the loss of their child, they noted significant changes within themselves, in the way they perceived their spouses, in the manner in which they related to their surviving children, in the kinds of friends they enjoyed, in their faith—in short, in almost every aspect of their lives. The next five chapters address each of these areas in turn. This chapter focuses on the changes parents perceive within themselves, the alterations in their personal views of the world, the way they feel about themselves, about life, and about death.

As parents talked about their growth and the evolution of their view of life in the years following their loss, five different areas of focus became apparent:

- **Lost Innocence:** Parents experience a sense that life has lost its chastity or purity.
- **Changed Values and Priorities:** Parents' values modify as they search to reclaim a sense of meaning in their lives.
- **Perceived Control:** Alterations occur in parents' perceptions of the control they have over their lives.
- **Empowerment:** Personal efficacy is enhanced.
- **Attitudes Toward Death:** In changing their attitudes toward death, parents change the way they approach life.

Excerpts from the interviews highlight the ways in which parents find themselves altered in each of these areas.

Lost Innocence

The fissures in the forest floor following an earthquake, the Garden of Eden following the taste of the apple, both are analogous to the modified panorama in the aftermath of acute grieving. The verdant forest and the lovely garden remain the larger contexts for life, but the features alter, become less perfect, less idealistic, and mellowed by wisdom. Life becomes good again. Pleasure returns. The hectic pace resumes. Yet . . .

> Truly I am living life to the fullest. I've made a way for the pain and the full life to co-exist. You can have both. It's like going to a party with a toothache. The real healing is when you accept that the pain is always there. It has changed the way I define myself. Formerly I might have called myself a

journalist, or a mother; now, first and foremost, I'm a bereaved parent. That's what I feel is the most important and prominent part of who I am.

Veronica

I listened to Veronica tell the tale of her transformation and smiled at her image of "going to a party with a toothache." Her phrase seems to capture the essence of the theme of the loss of innocence that is expressed by so many of the "old" bereaved. When the early ravages of pain subside, a dull ache remains in the far reaches of awareness, a reminder that life can never have that blush of perfection again.

Youth is idealistic and invulnerable. Teens take risks that make the older and wiser cringe. The innocent see death as a distant abstraction, something that has nothing to do with their real world. Life is in control. Life is orderly; actions produce predictable results. When a child dies, that idealism shatters, like Humpty Dumpty, never to be put back together again. Whatever happened to the rose-colored glasses? All of life is suddenly different, forever.

Here are the words of the parents as they talk of that lost innocence.

This life started for me on September 8, 1987. It's hard to remember what life was like before. I look at pictures of me before and there is a stranger looking back. This person I am today has lost all innocence. I knew that children died; but I thought only other people's children died. I had a total expectation that life went on in an orderly way. Even though I lost my brother and my mother and my marriage broke up, I never really knew. It never crossed my mind that you could lose a child.

When I think about Tanya's death, I am always amazed that it can hurt so much after so many years, that the pain can be so raw, and that I can still feel happy again at the same time. After eight years, I still need to be reminded and reassured about how far I've come in reorganizing and restructuring my life.

Veronica

You live with the fact that you will never feel pure joy again. It will always be tinged with the sadness of longing. Every happiness is weighted. It's like a vise slowly squeezing your heart. Whenever you feel happy, you remember that your child isn't here to share it, that she isn't here to have the joy in life she deserved to have. It's always that minor chord intoning in the background.

Margot

One of the component pieces of the idea of the loss of innocence is the reality that the skies are never again crystal clear; the possibility for purity and perfection is gone. Clouds hang overhead in a way they never did during the age of innocence when perfection was still possible. The clouds may be out of view at any given time, but they hover and reappear unbidden.

Suddenly, here it is again. The chain of suggestion can begin almost anywhere: a phrase heard in a lecture, an unpainted board on a house, a lamp pole, a stone. From such innocuous things my imagination winds its sure way to my wound. Everything is charged with the potential of reminder. There is no forgetting.

—Nicholas Wolterstorff,
Lament for a Son

For bereaved parents, birthdays, anniversaries, holidays, and weddings lose the unfettered delight they may once have had. Now these occasions are tinged with an element of dread. The wonder and openhearted pleasure of watching children open their Christmas gifts becomes a scene haunted by ghosts of Christmases past. The wedding of a nephew kindles thoughts of the wedding their child will never have.

When a "lamp pole" or "a stone" or "an unpainted board on a house" throws you face to face with the evidence of your loss, the clouds that hover threaten to unload their deluge.

The springtime really bothers me. Why couldn't he have died in a season I hate? The day he died, that whole weekend, as a matter of fact, was spectacular weather with bright blue skies. When the weather is like that it brings it all back. Planting and gardening bring it all back. It makes me sick inside. I can't enjoy a sunny day without the pain.

Barry

Regina found the cloud descending at the ninth anniversary of her son's death. He had died at the age of nine. It hurt her terribly to realize that he was now dead as many years as he had lived. The year brought the additional reminder that, "I should have been buying him a car this year." Milestones of all kinds trip up the bereaved parent.

We have seen how the death of a child is an expulsion from the land of innocence. As Veronica said, no matter how many losses preceded, how wise we were in the ways of life, this event, above all, shatters any vestiges of thinking that life is fair. That is not to say that these parents suggest that they become bitter or hard or pessimistic. That is not the case. They each express that over the years bitterness wanes; softness returns. As we will see, many later redouble their efforts to be kind, considerate, sensitive, and fair. The loss of innocence can become motive for greater compassion toward others in pain. But any vestiges of illusion about the rightness and fairness of life are simply gone.

Changed Values and Priorities

Victor Frankl, in a small, poignant book entitled *Man's Search for Meaning*, wrote about his experiences in a concentration camp in Germany. He described that the impetus to survive the Holocaust came from creating a reason to do so. The purpose Frankl set for surviving was for him to tell the world. He found scraps of paper on which he recorded his experiences and committed to memory the horrors he saw so that he could bear witness for future generations. The power of purpose to help people bear the unbearable cannot be underestimated. Perhaps our founding fathers missed an essential truth when they wrote that each citizen is entitled to "life, liberty and the pursuit of happiness." The "pursuit of mean-ingfulness" is more to the point, since it is through meaningfulness that one ultimately finds happiness. Many of the parents found that life lost meaning following the death of their child. One of the vital tasks of grief-work is to come to a point where life again takes on meaning. Parents who fail to find meaningful outlets remain stuck. Parents who seek and find meaningful pursuits heal themselves more quickly.

Bereaved parents gravitate toward others who are suffering. They often find that the initial bond of pain evolves into a desire to give care and support as their own anguish abates. Some of the parents who attend self-help groups to find solace and compassion during the early months of grieving stay on to become leaders in the group long after their initial need abates. "I stayed because it was important to help the newly bereaved so they wouldn't feel so alone," one mother noted. Parents find that helping others is grat-ifying and gives them a feeling that they are making an important contribution. Many said they participated in this research for the same reason; they hope to light the way for others so they can have an easier time. Coming to feel worthwhile again is one essential ingredient in healing. Often, the tasks parents undertake to renew their sense of purpose wind up enriching the world around them.

Jill exemplifies a parent whose grief propelled her toward humani-tarian pursuits. Jill "grew up in an alcoholic family." She married a man who became alcoholic and died at age forty-five as a result of his alcoholism. Her twenty-eight-year-old daughter "had problems with alcohol." After her daughter committed suicide, Jill endured a phase of numbness. She returned to her job but said she had the feel-ing that only her physical presence was there. Any commitment she previously had to her work was missing. She now found the work meaningless and banal. She was acutely aware of the toll alcoholism had taken on her life and decided she had to do something to battle a disease that had haunted her since childhood. She entered a train-ing program and became an alcoholism counselor.

Sarah's death was the final impetus. I had already lost my parents and husband to alcohol; but she . . . she was the love of my life. It was as if God hit me over the head with a two-by-four. Finally I knew that I needed to do something about this problem. I couldn't help my own daughter, but maybe I could help someone else. I had to do something meaningful with the rest of my life. I had to impose some meaning on this.

Now, six years later, I'm doing it for myself, but Sarah's death was certainly the impetus. I think maybe I can heal from this. When I see someone get help and progress, I think of her. It makes it just a little bit easier to accept. It wasn't meant to be that I stopped her. I used to think that if I loved her enough I could keep her alive. Today I know that you can't save anybody. But I know through the work that I do that sometimes you can help somebody to save themselves.

Jill

Many parents become absorbed in work that involves nurturing other people who are in need. They find they get the greatest sense of purpose from giving service or relieving the suffering of others. Among the helping activities the bereaved parents in this group became involved with are working in a hospital with babies with AIDS, volunteering in a shelter for battered women, serving in a variety of leadership capacities with TCF, becoming an alcoholism counselor, working as a bereavement counselor, conducting therapy groups for survivors after suicide.

Candy Lightener, the founder of Mothers Against Drunk Driving (MADD), is a shining example of how a bereaved parent used the energy fueled by her grief to make the world a little better. After her daughter was killed by a drunk driver, she found her only solace was to dedicate herself to the cause of raising awareness of the dangers of driving while under the influence of alcohol. She was a prime mover in getting legislation passed and in changing attitudes toward drinking and driving. She survived her loss by creating a new purpose in her life and provided a service to society in the process.

Margot plans to leave her job as a successful marketing executive. She says the job has no meaning for her anymore. She makes a great deal of money but feels empty. She is returning to graduate school to begin a new career in a helping profession where she can work directly with people and feel she is having a greater personal impact than she feels in the corporate world.

Along with an increased altruism and a sense of wanting to provide help to others comes a greater sensitivity toward suffering. Parents say their eyes are open to the pain in the world in a way they had not been in their more innocent days. They valued the support they received from loved ones during their grief and consequently became more acutely aware of their responsibility to give their support when others needed it. Repeatedly, bereaved parents spoke of a newly acquired value for empathy with the anguish of others. Here are their own words:

> The way I deal with people who are grieving is different. Now I know that it's necessary to talk about the deceased. I'll go up to a friend who lost her mother and say, "I loved the way your mother kept her garden." You don't run away from people who are grieving. It's important to stop and have some coffee and reminisce about the deceased in some pleasant way.
>
> *Cass*

> I'm a staff writer for the local newspaper and it's always been my job to write the obituaries. Now if there is a deceased child, I write a personal note to the parents. I'm more attuned than I used to be. I haven't become a better person, but I know something I didn't know before. This life is all we have. If you can ease someone's pain . . .
>
> *Betty*

> I have a friend who recently was diagnosed with colon cancer. I understand what it was like to get a call every day that someone was thinking about me, so I'm much more attentive to those kinds of things than I used to be.
>
> *Margot*

My brother died many years ago from cancer. Because I didn't have cancer, I couldn't understand him. Now I see my own blindness. If he were dying now it would be different. If my brother were dying today, I'd be more there for him.

Veronica

My daughter had had multiple miscarriages. I remember saying, "Oh, honey, there will be others." Isn't that horrible? I never realized how she must have felt when I said that to her. How horrible of me. How dare I say that to her! You don't know what to say, so you say what consoles you, I guess. I learned better after Stuart's death. People said to me, "Thank goodness you have your other children." I just felt, "My other children are never going to replace Stuart." Now I know better. I never realized that my daughter's feelings ran that deep for a child she never saw. But, of course, they did.

Gloria

Awareness of the need to be more compassionate and sensitive is one of the shifts in values we noted. Another value that undergoes an alteration is the manner in which these parents define success. Values placed on work, achievement, money, acquisition, and status all are reexamined through a different lens. With heightened awareness of the transience of life come changes in the way in which priorities are ordered. Values for time spent at work versus time spent with family shift. The fathers, in particular, reexamine work priorities. Many fathers conclude that their earlier value for work and achievement no longer has the same meaning.

I am where I always dreamed of being professionally and economically and it doesn't mean shit.

Bruce

I was a workaholic since high school. I worked sixty to seventy hours a week in the corporate world. When I was in my fifties I worried about having to stop work at sixty-five.

I had no hobbies. Then Tommy died and I couldn't care less if the plant burned to the ground.

Thomas

I used to be reluctant to take time away from my business. But for all the time Michael was sick, I had to take a great deal of time. Since I was away from business for all the bad reasons, I now am not going to miss any opportunity to be away for pleasant ones.

Russell

I worked a lot before Joel died; now it's not worth it. You need to make time and savor it with your family. So it's affected my job. I used to work nine to five; now if I can get home by two, I do. I want to see my kids grow up. I realize that my son was there and then all of a sudden he wasn't.

Barry

On the job everybody thinks everything is a crisis and a tragedy and they get crazy out of their minds from the chairman on down. I just say, "Did anybody die?" That seems to put things in perspective. If you can't tell me anyone's dying, I'm not gonna get crazy. Of course, there are the times I start to get crazy, but then I can pull that thought out and say, "Wait a minute. Nobody is dying." I didn't have that perspective before.

Margot

Time takes on new dimensions. The manner in which parents choose to spend their time undergoes a shift. Parents who placed a great deal of stock in working and saving for the future realize that the future is ephemeral. The seesaw balance shifts slightly; more is invested in the present and a little less in the future.

I've learned to live life one day at a time, work hard, play hard, because you don't know when you'll get kicked in the ass again.

Bruce

Climbing the work ladder, deferring today's pleasures for tomorrow's security, acquiring a home, a car, and a few creature-comforts are values typical of the American dream. All these values come into question. Career success and materialism come under scrutiny. A number of parents said they found they couldn't care less about material things.

> My husband, Rick, bought me a BMW for my birthday. It didn't matter to me. I was brought up poor and I used to think about how nice it would be to have beautiful, expensive things. Not now.
>
> A while ago Rick's son smacked up the car. I just told him not to worry. If it's something that can be fixed, it doesn't matter. If it's not death or cancer, it's not important.
>
> *Regina*

Not only do these parents say that their focus on "things" diminishes, but they find that materialism and superficiality in others becomes annoying. We will talk more about how this intolerance for superficiality affects social relationships in Chapter 7. Along with impatience for superficiality comes a sense of impatience with people who complain about trivial matters. Patrice says that she always has the feeling she wants to ask some complainer if she'd like to change places.

> I have no tolerance for pettiness. There are times I become abrupt and rude with people who complain about nonsense. This has made me tough. Nonsense doesn't bother me. Once someone smacked my car. It was inconsequential. I only mentioned it in an offhand way when my husband came home. It didn't matter. Before I was more materialistic. I cared more for clothes and makeup and looking good for others. Not anymore.
>
> *Patrice*

> I have a different way of looking at things. Like if I have a lousy day, I know it could be worse. Who cares if it's cold

outside after this happens? One day I ran into a woman in the neighborhood who asked me if I were the father who had lost a son. She went on to say that she understood because she had just lost her dog. After she said that, I didn't even want to get to know her. All I could think was, "Go out and get another dog, lady."

Barry

I don't have time for cocktail party talk anymore. I have no time for superficiality.

Karen

It drives me crazy when someone bitches about their kids.

Evelyn

I just can't spend time with someone who wants to complain that their furnace broke.

Pauline

I'm more brutally honest and impatient. Things I used to let go, I don't anymore. I'm intolerant when I see people hurting other people and I speak out.

Felicia

Many parents find their values changed; their increased awareness of suffering makes them more compassionate; the rudderless existence following their loss leads them to seek direction more purposefully; their pain ultimately makes them more altruistic. Priorities change; work and family have different value attached to them. Value for compassion, for getting the most from the present, and for helping others replaces materialism and superficiality. Bereaved parents acquire a wisdom and maturity prematurely.

In this chapter, we just scratched the surface in examining how values modify as a consequence of loss. Here, we explored the evolution of values within the individual. In later chapters, we will see this idea of altered values revisited in different contexts. Values within the marital relationship adapt, as you will find in Chapter 5. Values for family cohesiveness intensify; we will explore that more fully in Chapter 6. Values for friendships shift, sometimes dramatically; those shifts will be examined in Chapter 7.

Empowerment

> Suffering can be productive. We know that painful experiences of all kinds sometimes stimulate sublimations, or even bring out quite new gifts in some people, who may take to painting, writing, or other productive activities under the stress of frustrations and hardships. Others become more productive in a different way—more capable of appreciating people and things, more tolerant in their relationships to others—they become wiser.
>
> *Melanie Klein*

Psychologists deal with people with a lot of different kinds of fears and personal limitations. "I can't talk in front of an audience." "I've always wanted to go back to school, but I'm afraid I'll fail." "I can't ride in elevators."

We know for sure that all the psychological treatment in the world—talking, understanding, analyzing—won't get a person over a fear. It is not much benefit to understand why you're afraid to ride in elevators. You ultimately have to get into the elevator and ride it to the top floor. In the early days of behavioral treatment for intractable fears, psychologists used a technique called "flooding." They exposed the patient to a large dose of what he feared, let's say elevators. If you're terrified of elevators and are forced into one, you are likely to have a huge anxiety attack, sweating, heart pounding, gasping for breath, dizziness, the whole can of worms. But the body sustains that state of alarm only briefly and the reaction soon subsides. No one died. After the terror spends itself, the patient is standing in the elevator, shaken, but a survivor, knowing that he can endure elevators. Expectations begin to change; maybe it is not necessary to fear elevators. There are more humane and less traumatic treatments for fears, but, despite its inhumanity, the treatment usually works.

That's essentially what happens when a parent loses a child. They've been inhumanely thrown into the most terrifying ordeal, ridden it up and down its whole length, in terror, in anguish, in tears, and ultimately survived. They didn't want to get stronger, there is simply no choice; black or white, live through this or die. These parents aren't necessarily brave or strong. They don't face their fears courageously. They rail and scream and die a thousand deaths each day, with each reminder, with every picture, or song, or holiday. They crawl through each day and toss sleepless through the nights. And, years later, after the tornado has spent its wrath, these parents know they have survived and are less afraid. Only after parents are able to break out of the confines of the personal hell into which they had been plunged are they able to see that the fiber of their being has toughened.

In the words of Ronald J. Knapp from *Beyond Endurance:*

> Those parents who have managed to recover some mean-
> ing tend to develop a sense of omnipotence and invulnera-
> bility relative to life's other hardships. They come to feel that
> there are simply no obstacles that they cannot overcome.
> They believe that they have met the ultimate challenge to
> their own survival and they have conquered it. In the process
> of rebuilding, it tends to become obvious that the survivor
> has indeed encountered the ultimate tragedy and has sur-
> vived.

Becoming empowered, internally more secure, is a topic we heard often in our interviews. The theme has at least three major variations, as we listen to the undertones. One strain is that parents gain grit, fiber, muscle tone, something of that ilk. They are toughened for having walked over the fiery coals. As a secondary related melody, our parents say they are more assertive, more able to identify and express their needs, to give themselves the right to ask for what they want and to say no to what they don't. And thirdly, they have greater courage; they have more courage to face their fears; they are more able to enter unknown arenas; they can err and have that be okay.

Margaret Lipner, seventy-nine, had two miscarriages, and lost a twelve-year-old daughter, Susan, to cancer in 1946 and a forty-nine-year-old son in 1987, just a year after she became a widow. She speaks both literally and figuratively about the toughening power of adversity:

> I am getting older, and there is no way into my house without climbing steps. Every day I thank God for the steps; they will strengthen my legs. My stepfather died the same day as Susan. We had two funerals in one day. When I was going to college after Susan died, I learned that my brother was terminally ill. I told my professor that I couldn't take it anymore. He said, "You must do one of three things: Die; let it drive you crazy; or somehow come to accept it and move on." Apparently, I did the third.
>
> This adversity has been my load to bear; it has made me appreciate life more, and made me stronger. You can spiral down, fast, or you can climb up. I've chosen to climb. I don't take things for granted. I think every breath is a gift. I see the cup as half full. I force myself on days when I'm not wanting to do anything to go out and walk in the park. I tend to be satisfied with what I have rather than moan about what I don't.
>
> Yes, I'm still aware of the empty chairs at the table—my two children and my beloved husband. I have pictures of my lost children in the bedroom. I can look into their eyes every night through the glass. I miss the hugs.

From a woman in her eighth decade, who has been intimate with the agonies and ecstacies of life, comes perspective, wisdom, and shining optimism. Margaret epitomizes a positive approach to life. The stairs have truly strengthened her legs. Despite more than a fair share of misfortune, she focuses on the rewards in her life. Her power is humbling.

That notion of having toned-up emotional muscle resounds throughout the interviews. Many parents play that same refrain.

Who I am today is a function of losing Sheila. It made me stronger, braver, less afraid to tackle something different. I can do it. Even though I didn't want to be brave, I had to carry on and be a mother to my other children, and be a wife. There was no choice; I had to.

Barbara

Regina sat in her doctor's office listening as he prepared her for her upcoming surgery.

He told me everything that could go wrong, the whole list of possible complications. I stopped him in mid-sentence and said to him, "You know, I survived the death of my son. The worst has already happened to me. Nothing you tell me can scare me. I'll cope with whatever I have to."

Regina

There isn't anything ever that could inflict more pain or hardship. I never will be in as deep a pit as I was. Nothing in life will ever make me stumble as hard. I am absolutely stronger.

Charles

You have to cope; you just do. There's no other choice but to kill yourself. It's the only other choice you have.

Barry

I have gained a lot of inner strength. No matter what happens, I have to go on. I am a survivor. When you lose a child, you end up with that security. The end result is the knowledge that no matter what comes, I will handle it. I have handled the worst.

Arlene

There's not a thing on earth that will knock me down. You know how steel has to go through fire to get its strength . . .

Cass

An aspect of gaining emotional strength is giving yourself the right to be your own person. People who are assertive are comfortable saying "yes" or "no." They are respectful of the rights and feelings of others without sacrificing their own principles. True assertiveness reflects a quality of confidence and maturity.

In everyday usage, the words "assertive" and "aggressive" are sometimes used as synonyms. In fact, they are opposites. There are similarities in that both assertive and aggressive people recognize the right to ask for what they want. The assertive person does so with respect for the right of the other to refuse, or to have different wants. The aggressive person's style of asking comes across more as a demand and ignores the feelings of the listener. By definition, an assertive stance is a respectful stance. An aggressive stance is one that ignores the feelings of others and often looks angry, contemptuous, or rude. We heard both styles from the interviewees. Many parents felt that the hell they had gone through gave them the right to take care of themselves better, to consider their own priorities as paramount, to put their family first and foremost. Some other parents felt an angry sense of entitlement, that the hell they experienced gave them the right to elbow their way to the front of the line.

The assertive parents in this study radiated an aura of having paid their dues and earned the right to follow the dictates of their own conscience. They shed the feeling of being obligated to partake in activities just to gain points and please someone else. Not that these parents become selfish; quite the opposite; they give more of themselves, but more selectively; they give more out of a genuine feeling of altruism than to please others. Gaining maturity is learning to be true to yourself, your own values, your own priorities rather than filling roles that others have defined for you.

> I had to rethink what I wanted out of life. I realized that time was precious. I had spent all my time helping everybody else. Then I finally said, "I've paid my dues; now I want

something for myself." I traveled and did the things I wanted. I left the job I had been in for years and started a business of my own.

Karen

Josie's story exemplifies newfound assertiveness. With her friends, with her husband, in her interactions with the legal system, she took on a stronger persona. As I spoke with her, I was struck with her strong sense of self, of knowing what was right for her and finding the inner resources to pursue her chosen course. She faced the community, her friends, and her family with the same respectful determination.

I changed. I became more assertive. I don't put up with a lot of baloney anymore. You get very impatient with people complaining about just nonsense stuff. Their husband works late so they have to spend all this extra time with the kids. They don't have enough money. And I'm thinking to myself, "Gosh, you should have my life." That would stop people. Then what would they say?

A lot of people I used to see, I don't see that often. Other friends have told me, "They don't call because they think you've changed. You're different." A friend wanted me to do something for her that normally I would have done; she would have talked me into doing it. I think she wanted me to color her hair. And I thought to myself, "No, I don't have time. I have two kids and I'm having enough trouble just getting through the day without reliving my daughter's accident." So I said no. It was a big change in me. I was never nasty. I just say no more often.

About a month after, I said to myself, "That guy who hit her never even got ticketed. My daughter is in the cemetery; we're sitting here totally depressed; I saw him driving around town with the front of his car bashed in where he hit my daughter. And he never even got a ticket!" I had a friend run his license and found that he had been ticketed twice before for speeding, doing in excess of eighty in a thirty-mile zone; then he got into another accident after he killed my daughter.

That's when I started writing to the prosecutor's office. "How come nothing happened?" They'd tell me they were checking into it. I was going after this guy. I fought for a year. My husband didn't realize I had such a fighting side to me. He hadn't seen this in me over the years. He knew I was strong, but I think he was surprised at how strong I became. I fired the lawyer who failed to notify me of the time of the grand jury hearing. My husband said, "I'm not going to fire him." I said, "I am."

I'm more assertive with my husband too. If he doesn't want to do something, I can say, "Come on." He didn't want me to go back to school now because of the money. But I decided to go and I said, "I'm going." He agreed and we're managing.

Josie

There is nothing like hitting bottom to arouse the feeling that you might as well go for broke because there's nothing more to lose. Both Patrice and Theda took courage from that feeling.

With Sid's death I hit bottom. After that I feel I can deal with anything. I've had the worst. I don't have to please anyone anymore. I've been to hell and back again.

Patrice

Theda spent her adult life in a marital relationship in which she felt overpowered and intimidated. As a consequence of losing Jules, she eventually gained the courage and determination to leave her husband, Roy. Surviving her son's death gave her the impetus to change what was untenable. She would no longer allow herself to be subjugated.

Roy and I had been involved in ballroom dancing. We taught it. I tried to get back into it after Jules died, but I just couldn't. Roy insisted. He forced me. It felt as if I were dancing on Jules's grave. He pushed and I gave in. Today, with the strength I've gotten from having survived, I'd tell him to go to hell.

Theda

A number of parents said that one of the reasons they dropped out of self-help groups was that so many of the newly bereaved were angry. They spewed that anger like buckshot, at the society, at the legal system, at the medical establishment, and even at other bereaved parents. As we will note throughout, nice people get nicer and nasty people get nastier.

Betty recognized, years later, that what she felt following her son's death was anger that came out as hostility. With the wisdom of hindsight, she could see that during that period she stepped on a lot of toes. She seemed to have enough insight to pull herself up short.

All the guards were down. I didn't care who I offended.

Betty

Hand in hand with an increased assertiveness is a quality of courageousness. These parents could take chances doing things that previously had intimidated them. They could risk losing face, being wrong, making a mistake, feeling uncertain. They could risk these minor threats to their self-esteem because they knew they had survived a far greater assault to their being. The prevailing attitude is: "What could happen to me that would be worse than I have already endured?"

I'm much more definite at work, more willing to speak up at large meetings and say what I think.

Cass

Somebody asked me if I would speak to a convention in one of these big groups. My immediate reaction was, "Absolutely not! I can't speak in front of such a big group." And then I had a long talk with Marion and I told her that

I have to make some positive changes in my life. The chapter in my life before Marion died is closed and I have to do things that are different and daring. As a tribute also to Marion, I knew I had to do positive things. So I said, "Okay, I'll try it." So I got myself a course in public speaking and I did it. And I was scared to death. That's the message I've had. I didn't want to stagnate and become bitter.

Margot

Before he died I was a full-time parent. I would have probably gotten some sort of job eventually. When he died, my life turned a different path. That person I was before never would have driven into the Bronx. She never would have spoken in front of an auditorium full of people. She never would have gotten her master's degree. Now, in spite of the fact that I'm still afraid, I'll do it anyway. My son experienced a passage through death. I died when he did, not my body, but still a death. In order to get my life, and his, back, I had to go through the shadow of death rather than avoid it.

Donna

Becoming more self-assured and consequently better able to act assertively with friends and family are qualities bereaved parents see they have acquired as they look back over time. It takes quite a number of years for an awareness of these changes to develop. A number of parents who are older and more than a decade past their loss remark that they aren't quite sure whether to attribute their newfound strength and greater courage to the toughening power of surviving hell or to the process of maturing over time. Surely, many people become wiser and less intimidated with maturity. Life either toughens us or gets the better of us. Parents recognize that some maturing occurs as a natural consequence of aging. Nevertheless, they affirm that it is the effects of grief that set the strengthening process in motion. They see that the end product of their grief-work is that they become more definitive in what they value. They feel they have paid their dues and have earned the right to stand up for themselves. They see that the end product of the grief-work is that they are more self-assured.

Author and bereaved parent Harriet S. Schiff succinctly summarized the idea of empowerment:

> The fear of the unknown is behind us . . . because we have already taken a long look at hell.

Perceived Control

We go about the business of parenting by exercising due caution. Remember to bring a sweater today; take off those wet shoes; eat those green things; fasten your seat belt. It's comforting to imagine we have some control over our children's health and safety. But as vigilant as we may be, fate can intervene. No one knows better than Felicia and Rhoda how utterly impotent parents are to protect their children. Both these mothers had children who died suddenly from infections gone wild.

Asked how she now reacts when her surviving children become ill, Felicia says she reacts with a sense of fatalism. She is no more distressed than she was before her daughter died, perhaps even calmer. She says that she now feels a sense of helplessness, that what will happen will happen regardless of her best efforts. Rhoda, on the other hand, says that she becomes so vigilant and terrified that she is in a virtual tizzy every time one of her children shows the first sign of illness. Confronted with the capriciousness of life, each of these two parents reacts in diametrically opposite ways. One's level of vigil increases while the other's stays the same. Vigil is a mild form of anxiety. Perhaps the best description is the word "arousal," which says that the person goes into a higher gear and the adrenaline begins to pump a little faster.

Whereas Rhoda turned up the volume of arousal related to keeping her children safe, Felicia turned it down. As is the case with arousal, too little or too much can lead to problems. We normally live with an optimal level of arousal that keeps us on our toes and keeps our noses to the grindstone.

Let's look at the two extremes of too much and too little arousal to see where those roads lead. Too little arousal can lead to under-achievement. Think of the kid who doesn't worry about the test that's scheduled for Monday. He is free to spend the weekend play-ing hockey. But the kid who worries too much is in no better shape. He is likely to overstudy, spin his wheels, have trouble con-centrating, and waste a lot of energy.

The same continuum of too much to too little worrying applies to these bereaved parents. Rhoda has generalized from the horror of her child's death and now sees danger lurking everywhere. She is predicting harm in the same way a woman who has recently been raped sees a rapist in every dark corner. She has built a psy-chological torture chamber, climbed inside, and locked the door. It is difficult for her to discern "safe" from "unsafe." She, therefore, anxiously assigns too much to the category of "unsafe."

Fatalists like Felicia, on the other hand, have thrown in the towel. She has declared that the battle is over. She is defeated and helpless. She, like Rhoda, is unable to discern "safe" from "unsafe," but she automatically assigns too much to the category of "there's nothing you can do about it anyway." Since she is helpless by def-inition, there is little sense in trying anything. An exaggeration of "helplessness" as a style of thinking is one of the components that leads to depression.

Depression is thought to be related to feelings of psychological helplessness. There is a perception of having too little control cou-pled with a belief that nothing can be done to alter the situation. People who learn that they have no control over the most impor-tant aspects of their lives are at risk for becoming depressed. They are not steering; life happens to them.

People who have too much responsibility too early in life, who have to control more than they are able to control, often wind up excessively vigilant or anxious. Thus, extreme fatalism is associated with depression; extreme vigilance and overprotectiveness are associated with disabling anxiety. Fortunately, none of the people we interviewed had adopted either of these extreme positions on any enduring basis. The presence of either extreme calls for professional intervention.

The comfortable sense people usually have that life is predictable and controllable is thrown out of balance with the death of a child. Bereaved parents know that life can be thrown topsy-turvy without warning and without their ability to do anything about it. They know all too well that the "Sword of Damocles" always hovers and that they are essentially powerless to control its descent. Each of the bereaved moves some small distance toward either helplessness or hypervigilance. Some become a degree more cautious, some a degree more fatalistic. But all bereaved parents learn that, despite their best efforts, they are most vulnerable and least able to control the most important aspect of their lives, the well-being of their children.

Attitudes Toward Death

One of the important characteristics that separates the human animal from all others on earth is that we humans, alone, are capable of self-reflection and therefore have an awareness of our mortality. The fact of our mortality is almost universally viewed negatively. Death is associated with cobwebs, with evil, with suffering, with dread. Only in religious depictions is death portrayed with rays of light and welcoming open arms. More often death is draped in black.

In modern times, medical ethicists debate the morality of eugenics. Can death be merciful? Are there ever circumstances when death is preferable to life? It seems that death is getting better press now than it got in the past. Bereaved parents can tell you that death has lost its sting. Death embraces their child and they, therefore, come to view it in a very different light. We noted four kinds of changes in our parents' attitudes toward death. The first, wanting to die, is a very transient reaction to intolerable pain. The remaining three attitude changes are enduring. These three altered perspectives suggest: (a) that death loses its usual macabre overtones; (b) that death brings the welcome prospect of reunion; and (c) parents see subsequent deaths very differently forever after.

Some Wish to Die to Relieve the Pain

Thoughts of suicide overtook a few parents in those first anguished months. These parents didn't actually want to die. They just wanted to end the intolerable pain. Thoughts of suicide intrude during the early months of grieving. Gradually, the fire subsides and, with it, the wish to die.

> I think I felt like—"This is it." I wanted to give up. I thought, "All right, God; I've had enough now. Just take me too."
>
> *Jill*

> There were days when I would just close myself away and not want to see or speak to anyone. The family had people here with me all the time. I know I was suicidal. I saw a psychiatrist for six months. He talked to me and gave me medication. I felt responsible. My son was in my care when he was killed.
>
> *Patrice*

> I wanted to go with her. I didn't want to live anymore. I was close to killing myself. I wrote a suicide note. Now I understand suicide.
>
> *Felicia*

In each instance, the thoughts of suicide persisted only through the very early months. As was the case with Patrice, the family recognized the need to stay with her constantly to give her support and protection. Intractable guilt or thoughts of suicide that persist over time must be taken very seriously. Professional consultation can help determine the level of risk when the family is unsure.

Death Loses Its Macabre Emotional Overtones

Ronald J. Knapp interviewed scores of bereaved parents as part of the research for his book *Beyond Endurance*. We found essentially the same phenomenon in parents five or more years past their loss that Knapp found in the relatively newly bereaved. As he stated, "These parents eventually came to the point where they no longer viewed death as the enemy. Many saw that death could be a friend!"

Death is no longer a foreign and alien land. It is a place where their child resides.

> If I die, I die. I know somebody from that country.
>
> *Betty*

> I was very sick last week, but I wasn't upset. If I die, I die. There's nothing I can do about it. I don't mind going.
>
> *Felicia*

> When they found that tumor on my thyroid, I didn't care. I'm not afraid to die.
>
> *Regina*

Since a child who dies is still a member of the family, the surviving and subsequent children are well aware that a family member is "in heaven," or whatever the family's characterization. You will see in Chapter 6 that going to the cemetery, lighting memorial candles, seeing pictures and hearing stories of their deceased siblings, weaves death quite naturally and not at all unpleasantly into family traditions. When young children take part in these memorials, death is no stranger, but an inherent part of life.

> Not only do I not fear death, but my children say, "I can't wait to see what heaven looks like."
>
> *Rhoda*

Josie's children have always included their deceased sister in warm traditions. The little ones include Ginny in their prayers, are taken out for a special dinner celebration on Ginny's birthday, play with toys they know belonged to her, and quite comfortably integrate their deceased sister into their family life. The little ones, born subsequent to their sister's death, drew a picture of the family that included Ginny in the sky walking a puppy. The whole family has an easy familiarity with death that seems quite unique to families who have lost a child.

Death Offers the Prospect of Reunion

Regardless of religious affiliation, a striking number of bereaved parents say they are *absolutely* sure they will see their child again. We will cover the subject of belief in reunion more fully in Chapter 8. Here, it is sufficient to note that the prospect of reunion softens negative associations with the thought of dying.

> I believe I will see Joel again. That's a comfort. I don't know if I believe it because I was taught it, or because if I didn't believe it I'd jump out a window. I need to believe we will be reunited.
>
> *Rhoda*

Belief or wish, the prospect of reunion offers hope to bereaved parents that allows them the mind-set to enjoy this life as a kind of way station until the joyous day when they will embrace their child again.

At one TCF meeting, I listened as a young mother humorously described her reaction to a toast to "long life." She said that she wished for a happy and healthy life, but having a long life would mean a longer time until she could see her son again. She was not depressed. She had no wish to die. But dying held the warm and welcome prospect of a reunion complete with wonderful images of that first hug after so long a separation. I can well imagine being at death's door and reaching out to grasp my son's hand. Even for a nonbeliever, that's a compelling draw.

Parents View Subsequent Deaths Differently

If your son is in Chicago and your brother is taking a business trip to that city, you will surely orchestrate a get-together. You want your brother to report back on how your son is really doing. You want your son to have the warmth of a visit from home. It's an occasion for sentiment. If your son is in heaven, and it is unthinkable to many bereaved parents that he is not somewhere, you make the same plans for when another loved one may be coming. You find yourself being somewhat comforted knowing that your child and your loved one will have each other for loving company.

> When my sister was dying from cancer, I would talk to Perry every day and say, "Aunt Marcy is coming." I wanted a sign from Perry that he would help her through the transition. I looked for a sign that I got through to Perry. Just at that moment there was lightning and a crash of thunder. I cried!
>
> *Bruce*

> When my father died I was relieved that Kevin has somebody with him.
>
> *Regina*

Since death is no stranger, and grief an all-too-familiar acquaintance, it is easier to relate to others who are grieving.

> I deal very well with death now. I try to help bereaved people. When I see people who have lost someone, I reach out to them. If they want to talk, I listen; if they want to listen, I talk; if they want to cry, I cry with them.
>
> *Arlene*

Just as Californians learn how to deal with earthquakes and people dwelling in a flood plain know how to prepare for floods, bereaved parents learn to deal with bereavement, their own and others'. They have a greater sensitivity to what words are right to say and what clichés ring hollow; they have a better sense of when to talk and when a quiet presence is needed. They are sought by the newly bereaved, who see in them a kindred spirit.

Summary

It is impossible for an earthquake to leave the earth unchanged. Features of the rivers and mountains, of the trees and the buildings, are all rearranged into a new order. Yes, order is restored and harmony returns, but some structures need to be replaced; rivers find new courses, mountains get a little taller or a little shorter as a consequence. So these parents portrayed the course of their lives. Life forever after is a wiser, more knowing life. Eyes are open wider; colors become more muted. With wisdom comes a shift in values. Priorities change. What seemed important in the days of innocence seems less so afterward. Parents seek activities that will lend meaning to their lives, no longer content with working exclusively toward material goals.

Having landed on their feet after being thrown to the ground gives parents a sense of power. They see in the mirror a person who is a survivor. That knowledge gives confidence; the confidence becomes self-respect; self-respect translates into assured and assertive behavior. Being assertive leads to increasing self-assurance. The more you behave confidently, the more respect you have for yourself; the more respect you have for yourself, the more you elicit from others; the more respect you receive, the more easily you are able to act affirmatively in the future. Many of these parents expressed that they experienced that kind of upward spiraling of confidence.

Reasoning that no one or nothing in this world could hurt them more than they have already been hurt, numerous parents say they become more willing to try things they have previously been afraid to do. They become more courageous at work and in relationships, able to take emotional risks with the knowledge that failure would not be devastating. They already have proof that if they were to be hurt they could endure and regroup.

Part of facing life squarely is being able to face mortality. Perhaps knowing the brevity of life makes one work the harder to reap the rewards of life. For bereaved parents, death is a place where their children reside; it is a familiar place, a place that also holds the promise of a welcome reunion.

As each milestone is passed, as the anniversaries and holidays add up over the years, as houses are sold and new ones occupied, the sharpest features of the landscape gradually begin to take on gentler edges. Just as the fissures on the fault soften with the erosion of time, so do the harder edges of the changed terrain of life after loss. Though the clouds hover, the reminders threaten, the toothache aches, they all mellow over the years. As time progresses, anniversary and wedding days become more difficult in the anticipation than in the actuality. In later years, the anniversary date frequently gets absorbed into the press of the day's car pools and chicken pox. Though the date is anticipated and noted, it can remain as background to the main events of the day without the acute stab of pain that is inevitable in the earlier years. Life becomes pleasurable despite the sadness.

Where this chapter documented the changes that parents perceive within themselves, the next four chapters document the changes they see in the way they relate to their spouses, their families, their social relationships, and their faith.

Chapter Five

Mourning in Marriages

This grief, Theodore realized, was one of the few separating
things in their life together. He couldn't help Suzannah here;
he couldn't reach her. This particular part of her had died. If
she had wept and grieved, he could have comforted her; the
ground would have bloomed again. But it was a sealed-over
area no one could reach, where nothing would ever grow.

He learned then about the isolation of grief, even for those
in the same grief. Grief can't be shared. Every one carries it
alone, his own burden, his own way.

—Anne Morrow Lindbergh, *Dearly Beloved*

Myths

You know, 70 percent of marriages break up after the death of
a child," one mother said with an air of resignation. I've heard
so many newly bereaved parents quote that prophesy of doom and
express fear that the tragedy of the loss of their child will be compounded by the demise of their marriage. The myth permeates the
popular literature, winds through the mass media, and gets passed
around by word of mouth. I don't know where these numbers
originated, but they are repeated with a great deal of regularity and
a great deal of assurance. I nodded my head in agreement, having
heard the numbers quoted so authoritatively so often that I
believed them, too.

When this study was completed and we found a low level of divorce or separation among the parents we interviewed, I set about asking myself how this group of parents differed from the "norm," the norm being all those bereaved parents who wound up divorced. Perhaps this group of volunteer interviewees was more stable, more intact, healthier than the general population. That made sense. Yes, that was it. This group was at the high end of the mental health spectrum. I was so caught up in the 70 percent myth that I felt I had to justify why this group did not conform to it. It finally dawned on me that perhaps the myth may be a particularly compelling fiction.

What the Data Shows

When I began to investigate the question of the divorce rate among bereaved parents, I found that the 70 percent statistics were from a few studies of small groups of parents quite a number of years ago. Those studies were biased and as full of holes as a chunk of Swiss cheese. Yet, somehow, they captured the imagination and became folklore. I then did a computer search of the bereavement studies in the mental health professional journals and found no definitive studies that assessed divorce rate among bereaved parents. There are a few scattered studies in which small numbers of parents were assessed, but those few parents can hardly be considered representative of the broad range of bereaved parents. The only reasonable conclusion is that the percentage of parents who divorce following the death of their child is simply not known at this point.

A 1984 psychological study of forty parents who lost adult children in automobile accidents about two years previously said that many parents reported that the quality of the marital bond had improved compared to the year before the death of their children.

Another study of twenty bereaved couples noted an emotional separation in the early months based on "the highly private nature of grief . . . that resulted in a virtual cut-off of communication." The researchers found that there was a loss of sexual intimacy in the early months. Bereaved parents were "mad at the world, at

God, at themselves," and irritable with each other. The study concluded that "couples withdrew from each other . . . because of their own intense anguish and because of their desire to avoid increasing their spouses' pain" (Reiko Schwab). But they did not find that those early problems persisted, nor did they find a high rate of divorce or separation.

I wouldn't even print the percentage who divorced in this study lest someone quote it or take it seriously. The Compassionate Friends (TCF) members who volunteered to be interviewed are not representative of all bereaved parents. People who attend TCF are likely to be particularly outgoing, to live near urban centers, and so forth. People who elect to participate in scientific studies are different from people who choose not to participate. They may, for example, be more willing to examine their innermost feelings and more willing to reveal those feelings to a stranger. They may be more inquisitive or altruistic. These differences make the studies inherently biased and the numbers therefore suspect.

What This Study Found

Numbers present only a slanted picture of what actually goes on. How would you count the couple who divorced after the death of their son only to remarry several years later? All manner of variations on the theme take place with no way to account for the variations in any numerical way. There are two women in this study, Brenda and Evelyn, whom you will meet shortly, who say that they remain nominally married, still share a roof with their husbands, but are otherwise totally estranged. They don't share a bed, meals, social activities, or even visits with their surviving children. Pension and Social Security checks won't stretch to allow them to live separately. There is the convenience of having someone around who can fix the furnace. But their separate grieving ultimately undermined closeness to the point that they could find no companionability. If I were interested in statistics, I would have to count these estranged couples as still married, yet that would surely be misleading.

We were very supportive and worked together as a team throughout our son's illness. But after he died, we started to not support each other. I went to a psychologist a month later and it was a big help, but Hank wouldn't go. We argued over stupid things. Hank's reaction was that he no longer gave a darn how he looked, how he acted. He didn't care; nothing had meaning for him. He says he can never have a good time like it used to be.

I resented the fact that he'd wear dirty clothes and didn't bother putting them away. Even though the psychologist explained that to me and told me that he was grieving in his way, I still resented it. We used to have a good marriage. But he's retreated and I can't handle that. He says he can't stand happy occasions like weddings. He won't go on ski trips with the group I belong to; so I go alone.

Evelyn

My husband and I are estranged. Paul's death destroyed my family. My husband wouldn't talk. He got nasty, which was not like him. We separated for a year and he went off to India to live with a guru. He quit his job and went from one project to another. He's still floundering. He can't support himself. We live in the same house but there is no marriage. If I closed my eyes, it would be a blessing.

Brenda

Evelyn and Brenda describe marriages that shattered emotionally but stayed together physically. Other couples live separately but don't bother with the formality of divorce proceedings. There are couples who divorce soon after the death of their child who say that the death had little to do with their parting, except perhaps to hasten it. Divorce was inevitable prior to the loss. There are couples who divorce a decade later who attribute the marital disintegration to the death of their child. There are no hard and fast rules. No one has a script. Couples seem to write the script as they go along, some for better and some for worse. These myriad permutations and combinations don't lend themselves to being counted. All in all, after the death of a child, marriages seem to go through the same hills and valleys as any other marriages but, perhaps, in an exaggerated form.

In the majority of cases in which bereaved parents divorce, the death is only the last straw in the demise of the marriage. Marriages don't die with the death of a child, but they sometimes receive an overdue burial. If parental bereavement leads to divorce, it may be all to the good. The death of a child causes parents to reexamine all aspects of their lives. Since they have less energy, they must consider where to invest the reduced energy they have. If they have to use their limited resources to cope with the griefwork, there is little left to cope with the repair of a floundering marriage. If they have to learn to live without the child they adored, they can readily learn to live without the spouse who adds little to their lives.

Some relationships sever because the child was the primary bond. There may have been no real marital companionship. As Katherine F. Donnelly put it, "Couples who separate may have been more parents than they were marriage partners." They separate because their marriage was troubled before the loss and there is no longer any reason to remain together. The child was the only glue that held them together.

A general perusal of the research as well as our own observations of TCF members suggest no dramatically greater tendency toward divorce or separation than in the general population. Problems that become acute during the early months appear to resolve slowly over time with no lasting damage. Often, having worked through these wrenching times together, the couple feels more positive about their relationship in the long run.

The overall thrust of this book is to examine long-range transformations that come about after the loss of a child. Just as individuals evolve through subtle shifts in their philosophy of life, in their values and priorities, so do marriages. Spouses perceive one another differently and dance with one another to a modified tune. The separateness that exists in early bereavement dissipates; the marriage grows back to its familiar patterns, modified only in its nuances.

First, we explore major differences in the styles of grieving of men and women and how those differences affect the marital relationship in the early bereavement. Next, we explore some pitfalls couples encounter as they navigate through their grief. Finally, we note the ways bereavement reshapes the marriage.

Differences in Male and Female Styles of Mourning

This culture has traditionally taught men and women to express themselves differently and to grieve differently. In couples there is often one who is more outgoing and one who tends to be more retiring. In Western society, women are more often expected to be the affective ones and men to be the more cerebral ones. Women are more inclined to seek interpersonal contact than men. Women learn to express feelings openly and men to keep them close to the vest. While women are no more likely to develop emotional problems than men, the majority of psychotherapy patients are women. This may be because men are expected to be strong and silent whereas women seem to seek interpersonal methods of solving their problems. They are more inclined to be in touch with their feelings and to be able to put them into words. Of course, these are not hard and fast rules. They apply only some of the time. In a sizable number of cases, it is the man who is the more expressive, the more outgoing, the one seeking interpersonal contact. To be sure, as author Ann K. Finkbeiner notes, "the differences in the way individuals grieve are greater than the differences in the way the sexes grieve." But for the sake of simplicity, when we talk about differences in styles of grieving, we shall talk about the women as being the more expressive and more apparently deeply distressed, though that is only a majority and not a rule. It is important to make it clear that we are not equating what is usual and in the majority with what is normal or right. Keep in mind that while one member of a couple is usually more expressive than the other, in any given case that can be the man or woman.

Traditional at-home mothers spend more time with the children. The daily routine of mother and child is more intertwined than that of father and child if the mother does not also work outside the home. Because mothers are with the child much of the day, there are many more reminders that stare mothers in the face after the loss of their child. Quite a number of mothers I interviewed said that going to the supermarket in those early months was unbearable. Passing the peanut butter or the cornflakes brought the grief flooding back. What mother goes to the supermarket without picking up the kids' favorites? It's such an automatic part of the shopping trip that you never give it a second thought until you're faced with the cold reality that Johnny won't be home for dinner.

At present, one of the factors that contributes to the different ways in which men and women grieve is the degree to which each is invested in the parenting role. It will be interesting to see if the style of grieving changes as a consequence of men becoming more parental and women becoming more centered on careers. For the present, it is necessary to report what we observed: women, in general, grieved more deeply and for a longer period of time. This observation is undoubtedly colored by the fact that the average current age of the parents we interviewed is fifty-six. They reflect the lifestyle of a particular generation.

Mothers talk about the difficulty they have going to bed without having kissed their child good night. They talk of the agony of setting the dinner table with one fewer place. They talk of the ghostly quiet around the house. They long for the car pools they once dreaded. Clothes shopping became gut-wrenching. Such hourly reminders are not mentioned by the fathers. Women are more involved in those day-to-day intimacies with the children. Reminders are literally everywhere. It is easy to see why wives feel resentment at their husbands for seeming less tormented and why husbands have difficulty truly comprehending the pervasiveness of their wives' mourning.

Greater Intensity

Therese A. Rando, author of *Grieving* and other important books about bereavement, found in her research that:

> Mothers and fathers will tend to grieve differently over time. For fathers, grief seems to decline much more rapidly

than for mothers. Grief tends to be particularly intense for mothers two years after the death, although this will diminish after more time has passed. This implies that the father's grief decreases while the mother's grief is either remaining the same or increasing. . . . It should be upsetting, but it should be recognized and understood as a normal phenomenon.

In a study of fifty-four parents whose children died of cancer, Rando concluded that "overall, mothers appeared to experience, or at least admit to, more intense reactions to bereavement and poorer subsequent adjustment than fathers," for periods up to three years following the death. Rando's findings were repeated by another researcher, Reiko Schwab, who studied twenty-five couples who lost a child and reported that "mothers were found to cry, read, and write on loss and grief, help others, and stay alone to a greater degree than fathers."

The present study, using different methods, different groups of people, and a lengthier time frame, supported the earlier findings that mothers experience more intense grief, on average, than fathers. We found that these differences between the parents contributed to marital divisiveness and an inability to comfort one another. Wives felt estranged from husbands whom they perceived as less bereaved. Husbands felt impatient with wives who were unable to move beyond their grief for long periods of time. Couples need to be forewarned to expect these differences so they can have more patience with one another and understand that the rift lessens with time.

Women tend to count the role of mother as being a larger part of how they define themselves than their work, social, or other roles. Men are more likely to count their work role as a predominant aspect of how they see themselves. Insofar as these factors apply to any given couple, it is not surprising when women see themselves as more bereaved than their husbands. They have lost a larger chunk of their identity.

Men, in this age group, had a larger investment in their careers. During the Great Depression of 1929, many men whose life-work disintegrated in the stock market crash jumped out windows.

When everything you have worked for your entire life goes up in smoke, there seems little reason to go on. With exceptions, men infrequently give evidence of the same overwhelming depth of feeling that was commonly seen in this group of women. Perhaps that difference reflects both that men are more defined by their work than by their emotional ties, and that their grief is more inward and, therefore, less observable.

The study of the relative contribution of culture and biology to the determination of sex-role styles is currently receiving a great deal of attention from social scientists. We know that both "nature" and "nurture" influence the development of personality traits traditionally characterized as masculine and feminine. In these changing social times, men are assuming a more central role in child care and women are assuming a more central role in the workplace. There is likely to be a resulting shift in how people define themselves, a blending toward the middle. Men will assign a larger piece of their identity to the role of "parent" and women will see a larger part of their identity as "worker." I expect that as sex-roles converge, so will the styles of mourning.

Differences in Emotional Expression

Another factor that adds to the mother's perception that the father is less bereaved is the traditional difference in the way men and women express emotion. Josie told me that after her daughter died, her husband never talked about her.

> I said to him, Rick, don't you care that she died? I had to keep talking about her. I talked about her with my sisters and with my friends. But the men didn't. They went outside and talked about baseball. It took a long time before I allowed Rick not to talk about Ginny and he allowed me to talk about her. I knew there was comfort I couldn't get from him or give to him. I knew my crying wasn't helping him.

Think of some of the expectations that society still places on men, despite our efforts at equal opportunity. Men too often feel obligated to appear strong, to act as protector, to be in control. They are expected by society to be self-sufficient whereas women are allowed to be more dependent. These expectations set men up to feel helpless because there is, in fact, so little they realistically can do to alleviate their wives' pain. If men have to mourn in private, it is no surprise that their wives might perceive that they are indeed grieving less deeply. Many mothers mentioned that they felt estranged from their husbands in the early months.

> In the beginning I was verbal and my husband was very quiet and to himself. He couldn't bear to see me so upset. He threatened to take Sid's pictures down if they were going to make me cry. It was very difficult. He didn't know how to deal with me. He tried to busy himself and not think. But Joe and I are closer now. It's hard for him to open up and now I can accept that. If we got through Sid's death, we can get through anything.
>
> *Patrice*

Their wives' open expression of grief often left the men feeling helpless. Since they didn't know how to lessen the grief, they often made attempts to lessen the crying. They became impatient with the seemingly interminable visible symptoms of grieving. In a rather futile attempt to calm the flood of feelings, Patrice's husband threatened to take down the pictures of their child, as if doing so would make the grief go away.

Trying to figure out how to bring comfort to a grieving spouse is made that much more difficult by the fact that the mode of grieving changes within any individual from moment to moment. Not only is one spouse different from the other at any given point in time, but each individual differs from one day to the next in where he or she is emotionally. So just when a spouse may be acclimating to their mate's mode of grieving, that mode may change. Grief does not progress in any orderly way. One day you go through picture albums longing for the sight of your child's face; the next day those same pictures are unbearable. One moment you need to be alone and the next you can't stand being alone. No one can know how to help you because you don't know how you'll be from one moment to the next. It is no wonder that two people who so desperately need each other's comfort often fail to find it in one another.

By the second week after Sid died, Joe went back to both his regular job and his part-time job. I still couldn't even feed myself or my daughters. I resented that he abandoned me. I resented that he could go to work and I couldn't even get dressed in the morning. My sister came to take care of me and feed the kids. My priest came and sat with me day in and day out. The priest kept telling me that I had to deal with this in my way and let my husband deal with it in his way. That saved my life and my marriage.

Patrice

Returning to work very soon solves several problems. Work can be absorbing and a good distraction. At work a grieving parent can feel useful and valuable whereas at home that parent may feel the opposite. Grieving partners are only sporadically able to be supportive of each other. At work, there is the hope of much-needed social support. In short, work provides a place to find refuge and nurturance. The ones at home, however, feel abandoned when their spouses return to work quickly. Secondly, at-home partners sometimes erroneously assume that returning to work is synonymous with lack of caring when, in fact, it may signify a very adaptive method of coping.

A couple's customary pattern of sexual intimacy frequently becomes interrupted during mourning. Men are more often likely to crave the comfort and escape that sex provides. They crave the few minutes they need to make them feel something alive and pleasurable. Women are more likely to find the thought of anything pleasurable—sex, social activities, entertainment of any sort—to be alien and to produce feelings of guilt. Couples resolve this difference during mourning in the same manner they have resolved it throughout their relationship. Most couples wait respectfully until they are both ready. A few husbands insist and seriously alienate their wives. Some wives go through the motions because they want to do something comforting for their husbands. Some wives go through the motions resentfully. Most couples gradually return to their usual pattern without detriment.

Potential Pitfalls

Let us explore three potential pitfalls that hamper communication and encumber the relationship during the early bereavement stages:

- the marital tango
- misperceptions and faulty assumptions
- unrealistic expectations

The following case history is fairly typical of the giant waves that threaten marriages in the early stages of bereavement. You can see the misperceptions and unrealistic expectations, the moving apart and gradual moving back together.

Min's story: A marriage that survived

That first year has to be what hell is like. I didn't care what happened to me. I had heard that 70 percent of marriages broke up after the death of a child, but I didn't care. Curtis was not there for me and I probably wasn't there for him. We were at each other's throats that whole first year. I almost hated him in the beginning because of the arguments he and our son had had. I found fault with him and said some awful things to him that I regret when I look back. I thought of leaving but there was no place to go.

Three months after our son died he accepted an invitation to play golf with his buddies. They thought he needed some distraction. I thought, "How could he go out playing golf and partying with his golf buddies just three months after our son died?" I couldn't see that golf was his way of dealing with his grief. Besides, he left me alone in the house when he was out with the guys drinking and partying. I expected him to be there for me. I had no perspective that this was his way of coping. I was so angry that he went to play and that he left me all alone that I called my sister and went to her house to spend the rest of the weekend and never told him where I was. He was frantic.

That first year Curtis started drinking; I thought that there was no way I'd spend the rest of my life with an alcoholic. He couldn't deal with the grief. I got the comfort I needed from the people at TCF. He must have gotten anesthesia from his drinking or hidden from his grief behind his golf buddies. I don't know how we survived. We went on like that for a long time, maybe five years, I'd guess. But the marriage came back okay. My husband was patient; he hung in there; he controlled his drinking. He can't express his grief. I learned to accept him the way he is. Our marriage is good now. I don't look at the little things anymore.

Min's story exemplifies some important points about factors that throw marriages into turmoil following a child's death. She describes how isolated they each were, how each grieved so very differently that they couldn't comfort or even respect one another. That profound sense of isolation is very common and well documented. Joan H. Arnold and Penelope B. Gemma, bereavement researchers, wrote:

> Grief is staggeringly self-centered. I sometimes feel a sense of sadness for the too many lonely days that might not have all had to be if we had known that simple truth. . . .

The Marital Tango

Every relationship is a dance. When one moves forward, the other responds in either a like or opposite way. Come closer; move apart; keep in rhythm. Couples have to evolve the steps of their tango, how much closeness is optimal, how much is too much or too little. They have to find a tempo that suits; the more quiet one and the more outgoing one need to adjust their tempos to keep time with their mate's.

Opposites do attract, the fast dancers and the slow. People whom psychologists call "stimulus seekers" often do match up with more serene mates. When you think about it, it's reasonable that a quiet, pensive, inner-directed type might enjoy the company of someone more bouncy. And someone who likes the lime-light and spontaneous activity might welcome the steadying influence of a quiescent sort. Of course, most people are a mix-ture of both styles, but nevertheless they tend to lean predomi-nantly toward either the outgoing or more introverted style. We call these opposites in personality style "pursuers" and "dis-tancers." Pursuers, as the name suggests, tend to move toward people; distancers have a tendency toward more solitary ways and move away from people. Pursuers talk; distancers listen. Pursuers enjoy noise; distancers prefer quiet. Pursuers take risks; distancers seek the safety of order and predictability. Pursuers spend; dis-tancers save.

Of course, these characterizations are extremes and all of us have a little of each. And the ratio of pursuer and distancer with-in each of us changes with different relationships and different cir-cumstances. Thus, a person may be more of a pursuer with one friend and more of a distancer with another. Pursuers and dis-tancers often marry each other and find a pleasant equilibrium over time that enhances both. However, an event as shattering as the death of a child can readily disrupt the established balance. As the stress intensifies each partner's personality characteristics, the distancer will need more privacy and solitude while the pursuer will need more company and support.

A fuller explanation of how pursuer/distancer personality dif-ferences disrupt marriages following loss is in order. Pursuers and distancers are likely to be opposed in how they approach many of the tasks of grieving:

- one may pull into himself while the other reaches out for support
- one may hide in activity while the other is immobilized

- one may wear his heart on his sleeve, mourning visibly, while the other carries the burden in stoic silence
- when one may want to find distraction in some entertainment, that avenue of solace may be anathema to the other
- frequently one spouse will need to talk about the deceased child when the other needs not to
- one pores over pictures and the other wants them out of sight
- while one may need the intimacy and comfort of sex, the other may not be ready
- one seeks social activities sooner than the other
- one wants to return to work much sooner than the other

Problems caused by differences in personality styles of pursuing and distancing show up with great frequency in marriage counseling offices. Counseling is usually the pursuer's idea, and that partner does more of the complaining, while the distancer is rarely the one to seek out the counseling and just wants to be left alone. To see the dimension at work, I'll use the example of Margaret and Hugo.

It is easy to tell the players without a scorecard from the moment they sit down. They sit side by side on the sofa, Hugo facing forward and Margaret angled toward Hugo with a hand resting on his knee. Hugo sits quietly, waiting for the action to begin. The opening silence doesn't last long. Margaret starts talking. She doesn't feel loved or valued. Hugo spends long hours at the office and on weekends he's involved with the volunteer firefighters. He often stops on the way home from work to chat with some buddies at the firehouse. He never calls her during the day and sounds rushed if she calls him. He forgets anniversaries. If she arranges a special romantic dinner, he is likely to eat quickly and retreat to the television. He falls asleep after sex, if he wants it at all.

Margaret and Hugo are a couple who have not resolved their differences in personality styles, or more specifically, the pursuer/distancer imbalance. The more Margaret feels neglected, the more she tries to talk, cajole, entice, all of which are pursuing motions. All of her actions are attempts to move toward Hugo and reduce the emotional distance she finds so isolating. Hugo needs more privacy, more emotional distance, and reacts to Margaret's attempts to bridge the gap by turning tail and running away, to work, to the firehouse, to the chores, to the television. The more he distances, the more she pursues; the more she pursues, the more he distances. The marital dynamic resembles a high-speed chase. The distance between the two doesn't change substantially. If one slows down, the other does, too. When either speeds up, the other follows suit. The purpose of the chase for each partner is to achieve the emotional distance he or she finds comfortable. But since that comfort zone is different for each, the chase is perpetuated.

Because mourning increases emotionality in pursuers and a need for solitude in distancers, there is a virtual guarantee of a cycle in which the pursuer speeds up the pursuit while the distancer speeds up the retreat in those couples who have not found a mutually comfortable emotional spacing prior to the loss. That cycle is set off because grief can't be a shared activity and almost inevitably leaves the pursuer feeling frightfully alone. The needy, hungry, lonely pursuers must understand that grief is lonely and isolating by its very nature, that moving toward their spouses inevitably causes the spouse to move away, that the only comfort lies in seeking solace from neutral sources and leaving the spouse at peace.

Misperceptions and Faulty Assumptions

If you feel leaden and barely able to function and your spouse is able to go to work, laugh, and participate in leisure activities, what are you likely to assume? Suppose your spouse also refuses to talk about the deceased child and wants her pictures put away. The most frequent assumption is that these behaviors signify a lack of caring or hard-heartedness. That is a dangerous leap of logic. These misperceptions, or bad guesses, are the initial step in a cycle that is self-fulfilling and ultimately confirms the misperception. The wife who sees her husband as cold, uncaring, or unfeeling when he returns to work soon after their child's death is likely to react to those perceptions. She may become more irritable, more demanding, and more accusing. In return, her husband will distance further. This, in turn, will furnish additional evidence of his cold, uncaring, and unfeeling nature. Wives are remarkably adept at getting husbands to do the things they find most annoying in their mate and vice versa. Wives who can't tolerate separateness drive husbands away with their demands; husbands who hate demands run faster and farther, thus inviting more demands.

Just a year after our son died, my husband was presented with a prestigious award by his colleagues for outstanding achievement and contribution to his profession in the preceding year. During that entire year, I counted myself lucky if I could drag myself through the demands of the day. The spotlight on his supreme accomplishments compared to my barely marginal functioning highlighted the difference between us and left me feeling utterly alone. At the award presentation ceremony where an audience of hundreds gave my husband a standing ovation, I stood in abject misery thinking they were applauding a fraud who didn't take a moment from his work to mourn his son.

In a dozen different scenarios I have heard those same misperceptions repeated by many bereaved parents:

He wanted to accept the invitation to a party. How could he want to go to a party so soon after our son died? I thought he couldn't have loved him as much as I if he could forget so quickly.

If he loved her he wouldn't have chosen blue for her coffin. She hated blue.

He got angry if I mentioned her name. He wanted to forget she ever existed.

What is so harmful to the relationship is to make negative assumptions about behavior that is different from yours. "He didn't care"; "He didn't love her," etc. The assumptions are often critical, judgmental, and almost always wrong. The motives you attribute to your spouse's behavior don't come near to hitting the mark. While a wife assumes that her husband's refusal to hear his child's name mentioned indicates his wish to forget her, it more likely indicates his wish to hide from his pain in the best way he knows how. Hiding may be a style that is quite at odds with how his wife copes. Nonetheless, the need to hide says that he, too, is coping with pain, not that he doesn't have pain.

In marriages that have a basically sound foundation, faulty assumptions are recognized as faulty even as they are staring you in the face. We saw earlier how Josie needed to talk about Ginny but that her husband needed not to talk about her. Here, Josie explains that as she felt the resentment toward Rick, she simultaneously recognized that she was making a mistake.

> After Ginny died, Rick never talked about her. I talked about her all the time with my family and friends, anyone who would listen. I guess what made it okay was that I allowed Rick not to talk and he allowed me to talk. I knew there was comfort I couldn't get from him and that I couldn't give to him. Of course, there were those times when I wanted to talk about Ginny and he didn't that I said to myself that he really didn't love her as much as I did. But I knew even as I was thinking it that that wasn't true. He just had one way to deal with it and I had a different way. I suppose that's a male/female difference.

Josie's story exemplifies two problem areas that frequently get activated following loss. The distance between the one who grieves more inwardly and the one who grieves more outwardly becomes greater; the tendency to think someone who is grieving differently is grieving wrong becomes exaggerated. Her words also exemplify how the self-fulfilling cycle can be avoided. She wisely notes that they each learned to respect the other's style and to accept the style differences casually as a "male/female difference."

Like Josie, Stephanie always assumed that her style of grieving openly, of seeking support from friends and talking it all out, was far healthier than her husband's style of stoic silence. She says that she had crucified her husband for the longest time with an assumption she later found to be false. She held on to her belief for quite some time, but by the time of our interview, some ten years past her loss, she had changed her mind. Stephanie says she has learned that silent, inward grievers fare no worse in the long run than their more expressive mates.

> Jesse always boxed his emotions. I resented that I couldn't talk to him about the child we made together. Jesse said that if he even began to let it out, there'd be no way he'd survive it. He was afraid to open those floodgates. He just closed down. I was jealous that he could put it out of his mind. On the other hand, I was sure that I was better off that I could talk and get it out in the open and deal with my grief. I thought he was shoving his grief down and not dealing with it so that it would come back to haunt him sometime later.
>
> With the perspective of time, I've come to see that he's no worse off than I am. Neither one of us has traveled farther. We're still separate in the way we remember. It's been nine years now and he never remembers the anniversary date. I wait all day for him to mention it, to give me a sign that he feels something. His silence drives me crazy. I mention it at the very end of the day because I can't stand it anymore. He didn't remember. That's all there is to it. He can put it away and not remember. It hasn't gotten me any further that I can't forget so I guess it's not so bad that he doesn't remember.
>
> *Stephanie*

Deciding that a different style of grieving is a wrong style is a very common misperception that encumbers a marital relationship in the early stages of bereavement. It is a faulty assumption when a husband decides that his wife is morbidly stuck and not trying to move forward. It is a faulty assumption when a wife decides that her husband is uncaring if he moves forward more quickly than she is able. Over time, most couples do what Josie and Stephanie did, accept the differences, respect the differences, and give their spouse the benefit of the doubt.

Unrealistic Expectations

Another general hazard that exists in marriages that is activated at crisis points is the tendency to expect too much from the relationship. There is a tendency to think that marriages can do more than they can reasonably do. People often have irrational expectations. Marriage is not an all-purpose relationship, meeting all needs all of the time. The best marriage can't fill all the social and emotional needs of the partners. Other family and friends, fulfilling work, and enjoyable leisure activities should all add enrichment to each spouse in addition to the nourishment the twosome supplies.

All too often, there are unrealistic expectations that hobble a relationship. It is so common in marital counseling to hear one spouse saying, "It isn't worth getting if I have to ask for it." Couples need to be reminded that a license to marry isn't a certificate in mind-reading. Some partners irrationally expect their mate to know how to make them feel better. Though couples get better at picking up each other's signals as time progresses, the strain of any emotionally charged situation can easily obscure either the signals or the pickup. It is unreasonable to expect that one spouse will know how to comfort the other. At a crisis point as traumatic as the death of a child, the pitfall of unreasonable expectations often opens into a cavern.

Feelings aren't reasonable. Often, people have feelings that they readily admit are completely unreasonable, yet exist quite powerfully. It is not uncommon for spouses to expect their mates to be able to make the pain go away. Though these expectations aren't reasonable, they nevertheless rattle around, cause resentments, and strain a relationship.

Margot's current husband is not the father of the child who died. She, therefore, does not expect him to be grieving as intensely as she. Yet, even under these circumstances, Margot feels abandoned and alone in the dark. Margot expressed the feelings of several women in this situation.

> Lenny tried to be of help. He was very supportive. But it bothers him to see me sad; so I have to wear a mask for him. I concern myself with how I have to be for him. He once said to me that I have to think about other things. I used to resent it, but I see where he's coming from. He's not bad, just incapable of understanding. There's that part of me I keep from him and that's why I rely on TCF friends so much. He just doesn't have a clue.

Spouses often expect their mates not only to grieve similarly, but to feel similarly regarding their religious observance. The admonition that "the family that prays together stays together" appears not to apply to the grieving family, at least as far as we observed. Husbands and wives are often divergent in the extent to which they are able to find comfort in their religious beliefs. There do not appear to be male/female differences. Sometimes the men and sometimes the women take more solace in religion. Expecting congruence is an error.

> My husband became religious and I felt that was a denial of reality. He was trying to find truth. He read to me from the Bible. He was trying to impose his way of grieving on me. I resented it at first. His religiosity lasted a long time. But I made a joke, a kind of parody, to show him how he sounded to me. We were finally able to laugh and it got better after that. I could deal with his need for religion if he wasn't trying to inflict it on me. We always had a strong bond. We can be angry but still know we love each other. Despite these religious differences, we've always had a strong marriage.
>
> *Pauline*

> My religious feelings became stronger after Sheila died. My wife is a lot less religious than I. Neither of us imposed

our beliefs on the other. Maybe we shouldn't be together on this. For me religion is filled with good stuff like respect for fellow man, things like that. It's okay that Barbara doesn't feel that way. We were two separate people before Sheila died and we are still two separate people. But she's 100 percent my partner in life. We will never separate.

Charles

Respect for individual differences across the board, not only in the religious sphere, emerged as a paramount factor in the successful navigation of a couple through the tornado of grief. Charles's wisdom in noting that he and his wife are two separate people who are partners for life highlights that vital dimension. A marriage is stronger if each truly knows that a spouse is not a clone. Accepting religious differences, accepting different styles of coping, accepting divergent needs without judgment, all signal respect. Acceptance, even in couples who are basically harmonious, gets derailed in the chaos of that early grieving period but most couples wend their way back to it slowly. The end result of increased acceptance is ultimately worth the trip.

Most of the parents we interviewed said they found their early support from sources other than their spouse. They found it in close family, friends, even acquaintances in the community, in self-help groups, in their religion, and in an assortment of counselors. There were a few instances of husbands and wives who truly clung together and derived solace from one another and who had enough emotional strength left to give to the other, but they were the exceptions. If machines won't work without fuel, neither will the human machine. A spouse who is depleted, without emotional resources, as most bereaved parents are, usually cannot be thoughtful, giving, considerate, a good listener, and utterly patient. To expect that is unreasonable.

According to Dennis Klass, a bereavement researcher:

> The death of a child has a paradoxical effect on the relationship between the parents. The shared loss creates a new and very profound tie between them at the same time the

individual loss each of them feels creates an estrangement in the relationship. The paradox of a new bond amidst estrangement is a central theme in the marital relationships among bereaved parents.

The paradox suggests that, because of the shared grief, parents are in the best position to support one another. It also suggests they are simultaneously in the worst position to support one another. Couples who find shared support are lucky, but somewhat unusual. In the long run, the ability to share support early-on is not a significant factor in the survival or solidarity of the relationship. Spouses who are unable to grieve in time with the same drummer come to a sound and healthy respect for their individual differences that ultimately adds flexibility to the roster of marital assets.

Ironing It All Out

What it all seems to come down to is that relationships that had a solid foundation of mutual respect may have been shaken, but remain standing in the long run. Relationships in which the partners are basically inconsiderate and self-absorbed continue to be so, or get worse, with predictable results.

We have stated previously that under stress "people become more like themselves," exaggerated versions of their best and worst characteristics. It really does make sense that under the pressure of highly stressful events, the simplest, most expedient way of behaving is the one that is the most practiced and, therefore, the most readily available. Under great stress one rarely has the luxury to evolve new solutions to problems, to try new and unproven ways of doing things. Under pressure we shift into automatic. Hence, we do what is easiest and most familiar.

During the most intense grieving, people who tend to pursue will pursue more; people who tend to distance will distance more. People who react to anxiety with an irritable stomach will be consigned to the bathroom; smokers will light up and light up again;

substance abusers will seek out those substances with a vengeance. People prone to depression will become depressed. If they have used alcohol like a medicine to dull depression in the past, they will drink more. All the weak links will be strained and some will snap.

In the intense period that follows a loss, the rough spots in marriages become sandpaper. The points of abrasion rub raw. There is a direct relationship between the degree of stress and the degree to which annoyances abrade. But as the intensity of the stress abates, so do the exaggerated personality characteristics and consequently the abrasion. People begin to settle back into their old skins. As months become years those early abrasions soften. Lessons are learned from the process: lessons about loyalty, lessons about expectations, lessons about pursuing and distancing dance steps, lessons about self and spouse.

The ability of partners to be emotionally loyal to one another is severely tested at a crisis point. The manner in which that test is passed or failed is a powerful factor in coloring the future nature of trust between the spouses. At a time of crisis, one spouse can either pull with or pull against the other.

Take as an example a relatively minor crisis such as a fender-bender car accident. How many women have you heard saying, "My husband will kill me." The wife perceives that her husband will turn against her and blame her for her carelessness in getting into the accident. In an opposite instance, the wife may rush home to a husband she expects to bring the tea and sympathy that will make her feel better. Escalate that crisis from a minor accident to the death of a child and you can easily imagine how each couple will dance an exaggerated version of its customary dance.

Blaming divides many a couple during crises. It's too easy to blame. We are trained to look for causes and to try to find reasons. Finding reasons is reassuring. Why did he get into that car accident? He was driving too fast. He was drinking. He shouldn't have been driving in the snow. Once we find all the reasons and assure ourselves that we would not have done any of the above, we can breathe a sigh of relief and feel safer for a moment. Finding reasons often leads to blaming. He got in the accident because he was foolish enough to go out in a snow-storm. She was raped because she was out too late, walking in an unsafe place. When such a completely unthinkable thing happens as the death of a child, people tend to look for explanations. If you were more careful, that wouldn't have happened. If you had-n't given him the keys to the car . . . If you had only noticed the fever sooner . . .

Blaming someone else can be an antidote for guilt. If it's her fault, it isn't mine. Blaming hurts relationships. It hits the blamed person when he or she is down. Blaming is a desperate attempt to avoid culpability, to get oneself off the hook. The blamer may get paroled temporarily only to find that he has greatly imperiled his relationship. Loyalty and trust are eroded.

Patrice learned a lesson about loyalty that has cemented her marriage. Blaming is one characteristic that seems to get dredged up and exaggerated during grief if the seed of it existed before-hand. Patrice recognizes that the seed was within her and express-es gratitude that it was not within her husband.

> Joe never blamed me for not taking care of Sid. It was remarkable that he never blamed me. He was remarkable. I thought he should have felt the anger because I would have. I would have said, "Why didn't you have him by the hand?" I guess that's why I know with absolute certainty that I can trust him. If my son had been in his care, I probably would have blamed him and it would have ended up destroying us. If we got through Sid's death together, we can get through anything. We have a very good marriage and we're closer now.
>
> *Patrice*

The marriage was solid before the death, but the simple fact that Joe didn't blame signaled the respect and loyalty that earned his marriage a lifetime bond. Like Patrice, Loretta felt the enormous weight of guilt when her young son died in a "freak" accident in their home. She blamed herself so harshly that she was overwhelmed with the thought that her husband would hold her responsible for failing to protect the child.

> The night that Kenneth died, my husband and I took a walk down the street. I told him, "I can't get through this if I think you're blaming me." He said it was just as much his fault because he was late in coming home that night.
>
> *Loretta*

With his simple act of sharing the burden of responsibility with his wife, Loretta's husband signaled his loyalty. At times of such profound emotion, these small actions of loyalty assume enormous power and come to symbolize the nature of the couple's bond. Loretta came to know, as she would never know under normal circumstances, that her husband was by her side. This couple recently celebrated their thirty-fifth anniversary.

Loretta's and Patrice's marriages gained strength because of the loyalty they received from their husbands. The bond was secured. Trust was enhanced. Their mates stood by them during the worst time, and therefore could be relied upon always. Few relationships are thus tested.

Going through this ultimate test reshapes the contours of the relationship. The relationship that emerges from the turmoil intact is often subtly altered. The marriage gains cohesion for having learned or relearned lessons in communication, respect, and empathy. In addition to gaining cohesion, other alterations take place. Cass looks back with keen vision and identifies a subtle shift in the relationship's power balance.

> Jess took pride in the fact that he was strong and decisive. He was out of town on business when Jaime was killed. I made the decision to donate his cornea. I made the funeral arrangements. I took care of what had to be done until he got home. The donation of the cornea was okay with him, but it bothered him that he wasn't part of the decision; it bothered him that I was able to do all these things without him. Even though he knew I was strong and he married me

because I was decisive and independent, this was the ultimate insult, that I could make all these decisions when he was absent. I think it changed the way we related after that.

Our marriage got apathetic. We grew apart in small ways. We changed from lovers to friends, like an old married couple. Jaime's death took the spark out.

Cass

Barbara can look back over the years and see that she gained a clearer insight into the manner in which she and her husband supported one another and learned what they needed from each other.

I found out that my husband is one of my children. I coped by becoming strong for everyone else. He needed me for emotional support. I gave it to him. I don't get what I need from him. But that's okay. There's no resentment. We have a good marriage and I know and accept the terms.

Barbara

In all, we saw only a few marriages that disintegrated as a consequence of the tragedy. Since in each case we have only the perspective of one of the partners, it is impossible to know the whole story. According to the spouse we spoke with, in each instance, the death triggered a mental breakdown in their spouse, an unleashing of earlier problems, and a virtual cessation of former ways of functioning. Some people break down and become mentally unhinged.

He dealt with it by traveling, taking ski trips, cranking up at work; a wall of silence came down. He would get hostile if I were to talk about our son. After about three years, he announced that he was moving out. He was angry and vindictive.

Donna

Marriages that ended had serious problems prior to the loss. The loss provided the impetus and the courage to escape. In some cases, marriages were secondary to the parenting roles and with the loss of the child that bound the relationship, the relationship quietly dissolved.

For most, marriages heave and quake and endure. Numerous spouses expressed the sentiment that, having endured the worst that life can impose, this marriage would survive. The bond is unbreakable. Couples who didn't know it before learn that it is vital to honor each other as individuals. They emerge the sounder and wiser for having learned that lesson. They learn the realistic limitations about what a marriage can and cannot provide. They learn they can lean on others outside the marriage without detriment to the marriage. They learn that even anger doesn't threaten the relationship if the anger is expressed respectfully. Many said simply that their spouse became a trusted and valued friend.

> Our marriage got closer and very intense. We will never separate. No one else could understand. We can get through anything. We're connected for life.
>
> *Felicia*

Caveats for Couples

- Different paces and styles of mourning are to be expected. There is no right way to do this grief-work. Your way is not better than your spouse's. You each have to design your own route through the maze.
- Recognize that a marriage is not an all-purpose relationship that can meet all of your needs all of the time. Much of the time you may be out of synch with each other and be unable to provide support. Finding support among other family and friends takes the heat off the marriage.
- Read nonverbal communication. If your spouse is silent, that is not a failure to communicate. That is a loud and clear communication. Respect it.
- Resist the temptation to become a mind-reader and assume what your spouse is thinking or feeling. Ask!
- Touch!
- Readiness for reentry into sex, social activities, or any pleasurable pursuit varies widely.
- Make a concerted effort to be kind, thoughtful, respectful, and forgiving.

Chapter Six

Family Relationships

Death of a child member becomes an important identifying piece of information about the family. It is woven into its
history and into the everyday operation of members' lives.
The child who has died continues to be a family member
after death. Parents are forever parents of a dead child as well
as of the surviving children. The dead child lives in memory.
The family grieves for him and remembers him with little
comfort and support from the society around them.

—Joan H. Arnold and Penelope B. Gemma,
A Child Dies: A Portrait of Family Grief

Amy was more than just a child. I was working out my
hurts with my mother through Amy because Amy got
along so well with her. She was getting from my mother
what I couldn't get from her. She made the connection with
my mother and father. It was so nice to see that special relationship with my mother because my mother and I didn't
get along. I was taking care of a lot of things through Amy.
Now it's all gone.

Felicia

As Felicia notes, a child is more than a child. The child is one step
in a dance pattern that includes each member of the family and
the combination of interactions among them all. That family is an
interactive system, in a way, like a country dance, stylized, with
steps and rhythms and variations on themes that are taught

through the generations. Amy danced not only in her own individual style but in time with her mother's rhythms and her grandparents' as well.

The family dance is greater than the sum of its parts, the whole having a personality that both reflects and influences the individual members. The dance has harmony, an interplay of melodies and movements. There is balance and structure that need to be maintained. When an event throws off that balance, everyone must scurry to reclaim equilibrium, to get back into step. The family, like the dance, has roles, rules, styles, communication patterns, expectations, alliances, and coalitions, all of which provide stability and predictability. Change any of those parts and the whole dance is disrupted. New patterns, roles, and alliances need to be established before the dance can again have harmony and beauty.

Before considering the death of a child as a specific event requiring massive family reorganization, let us consider the family as a system as it develops and adjusts to life's more ordinary exigencies.

Think of the changes in goals and interactions necessitated by the birth of a child. The unit has a new definition, a threesome instead of a twosome. Each member now adds a new definition, now including "parent" as a new role. The parents can't pick up and go out to the movies as they had. They no longer spend a quiet dinner talking over the events of the day. Even the frequency and timing of their sexual encounters must change. The blessed event creates turmoil that requires major readjustments in the way the original twosome relate.

And so it goes with subsequent children, each born into a family-created dance tapestry. The dance serves the traditions of the family and the needs of its members. It provides structure, meaning, direction, and identity to the new member. Each new arrival requires that time and energy be reapportioned; loyalties shift; competition for attention ensues. New alliances are made. Maybe the mother cottons more to one child and the father to another. Perhaps the older child resents the younger, forcing the parents to take sides. Roles are redefined. Husband becomes father; wife directs time and affection to the child, diluting what was previously directed to her husband.

From early in life, the child himself contributes to the development of his role, for example, by being shy or active or well coordinated. In our family, for example, we have jokingly assigned our three-year-old grandson the role of future barrister because of his continual attempts to argue us out of any rule we impose. A young child who is supposed to be the embodiment of her father's athletic aspirations has a fighting chance if she is well coordinated. If she is bookish and disinterested in sports, she must somehow be paroled or continue to be a disappointment to her dad.

Just as parents shape children, children shape their parents. The role, the position the child plays in the lives of the family members and in the family unit itself, is in continual flux. Just as there are multiple adjustments and realignments when the position gets occupied, there will be multiple adjustments, reverberations, and new balances needed if the position becomes vacated, that is if the child dies. If a family has difficulty coping with the anticipated developmental changes, envision the turmoil following a death. There is no preparation possible for the death of a child, even if the death is anticipated.

The family is a fluid system, adapting continually as internal and external events keep upsetting the rhythm, harmony, and balance that define its distinct interactions. Upsetting the balance upsets the orderliness and predictability of the behavior of the members. Dad changes jobs; he's more stressed and more irritable; he can't coach soccer anymore; now Mary can get the new bicycle they had been unable to afford; Mom has to pick up additional responsibilities; the whole system rocks and a new balance needs to be established. Even in the best of times, any shift in one part of the dance requires an adjustment of the whole; and any adjustment is stressful.

Even happy changes create the anxiety that comes with upsetting the apple cart. You know how a family reacts to the "joy" of moving to a bigger house. The kids grouse about having to take the bus to school. Sis complains that she can no longer ride her bike to play with her best friend. Mom worries about the higher mortgage. Dad sweats the lawn maintenance. It's not simple.

Consider the normal developmental changes that require the

family to reorder itself. Children grow up; milestones are reached; graduations, departures, and weddings take place in turn. Typically, these changes occur slowly with plenty of time and notice to allow for adaptation and evolution. Each change is integrated into the dance of the family. Where there is flexibility, these changes produce only minor interruptions in the harmony. When there is rigidity of roles in the family, the dance becomes clumsy and awkward.

The so-called "empty-nest syndrome" is an example of how rigidity of roles under normal conditions can become a problem. Children leave the nest with ample forewarning. If the mother is "parent" first and foremost, has no additional identity, has never emotionally weaned herself from the nest or the nestlings, the loss of the last chick is occasion for mourning and despair. Yet, normally, the empty nest is anticipated. Preparations can be made; courses are taken; social groups can be joined; the flexible mother adapts gradually to the changed equilibrium and new role definitions within the family.

When a child dies, the empty nest is far from a gradual, anticipated developmental event. It's as if a bomb were dropped. Each individual is forced to fend for himself; patterns of communication and interaction are blown asunder; roles and responsibilities are abandoned and new ones need be established.

The manner and degree of difficulty with which the family reconstitutes its unique patterns of interacting after the death of a child are determined by some of the same factors that influence its flexibility and resilience during normal times including: the mental stability and flexibility of each of the parents; the presence of other work- or health-related problems; the communication patterns of the family; the availability of social supports. Additional factors that are directly related to the grief-work are the timing of the death in the life cycle of the family; the role of the child in the family constellation; the child's relationship with each of the parents and siblings; the nature of the death.

How readily the family reestablishes an equilibrium will depend on these various social and emotional factors. Most important are the personal resources of each of the family members, their own mental well-being, their flexibility, their sense of self-confidence and self-worth, their ability to reach outside and trust others. A higher level of education is indicative of a person's stick-to-it-iveness, perseverance, and frustration tolerance and provides certain skills for problem solving that come in handy. Financial security plays a role in freeing people to work on the grief and reorganization without being sidetracked by having to invest additional energy struggling to meet the car payment.

Social supports are vital. The family in crisis needs outside supports as supplement when the internal resources are depleted. Extended family, friends, and community support make a profound difference. A family with aunts and uncles, good friends, a church group or fraternal group or garden club, is likely to be better cushioned in time of need than a more isolated family.

All too often, in these mobile times, young families are separated from their families of origin, to the detriment of all. Sickness in any member drains a family and stretches its resources. A family with stability, health, financial security, and social support can reorganize itself with greater facility than a family bereft of these resources.

According to Joan H. Arnold and Penelope B. Gemma, authors of *A Child Dies: A Portrait of Family Grief:*

> The family system changes when a child member dies. When a member of this system dies, the survivors must reorder the system, restructure it so that it continues to work for them. In a sense then, the energy for restructuring is part of the work of grieving, that is, it is energy needed to reorder one's life and integrate this loss into living and functioning.

The family's grief-work is the process of creating a new mosaic and new configurations that will establish a different harmony and grace. Next we will see how the families in this study went about changing their patterns of relating. We will see what they learned, how they erred, and what new family dances have evolved. First, we will take a look at the profound effects the family tragedy has on the siblings.

Siblings

We will address four major issues that families reported. First, guilt shows up in a variety of forms and disguises, often lasting for many years, waiting to be rekindled by the right spark. Secondly, surviving children often experience feelings of being emotionally abandoned by their grieving parents. The third theme is their loss of innocence. In Chapter 4, we noted that one of the enduring changes parents find in themselves is a sense that the purity and luster of life have been tarnished. Children, similarly, are tarnished and wizened, as we will see. Young children experience life at its most raw too early, leaving indelible imprints. Fourth, children are the innocent victims of the fallout from the emotional explosions within their parents.

Guilt

Guilt comes in a variety of shapes and sizes. The WW II Holocaust taught us the concept of "survivor guilt." People who survived the concentration camps asked over and over, "Why me?" "Why did I survive when people younger, healthier, smarter, or more worthy did not?" Following the death of a child, parents, and particularly grandparents, ask themselves that same question. "Why am I the one left living?" Siblings, too, come in for their fair share of survivor guilt. Since deceased children tend to be idealized, the surviving child and the parents may both silently ask, "Why this child and not the other?" We saw a number of parents who recognized in their innermost selves the feeling that they lost the wrong child. Brothers and sisters so often feel that the more beloved child died, especially as they witness the intensity of their parents' grief.

Survivor guilt can manifest itself in children as an excessive need to be good or perfect, worthy of being the one who survived. A child may try to take the place of his deceased sibling by adopting his unique characteristics or attempting to emulate the sibling. Or, conversely, he may be extra bad as a way to negate all those conflicting feelings.

When one child is seriously ill, the siblings may resent attention that pours out to their brother or sister and then feel guilty about their resentment. They may feel angry with their parents for being unavailable and then feel guilty about their anger. They feel guilty that they are having fun. They feel guilty because they want their sibling's belongings. These guilty feelings can last for years since they seem unacceptable and are, therefore, often not expressed. Children behave in a provocative manner, testing their parent's love and loyalty, and sometimes seem to be seeking punishment by behaving inappropriately. This provocative behavior can be an expression of guilt in which the child is unconsciously asking to be punished for harboring "unacceptable" feelings.

Another reason that children may engage in unacceptable behavior was reported by Therese A. Rando in her book *Grieving*.

> One adolescent decided to have trouble in school so that his parents would concentrate on him and get their minds off the pain of losing his sister.

Adolescents are in double jeopardy dealing with their own grief and the grief of their parents.

Tom, the father of a teenage son who had leukemia, said his daughter was pleased to be able to donate her bone marrow for her brother's transplant. When her brother died following the transplant procedure, Tom said his daughter remained distraught for two years:

> It was two years later when she learned that her brother died of pneumonia as a consequence of his compromised immune system and that, at the time he died, her bone marrow had begun to seed. Learning that he was actually beginning to benefit from her donation seemed to turn her around. She got better after that.

Gretchen, similarly, observed her daughter's prolonged guilt.

> My son's heart condition required that I give him a great deal of care. He was in the hospital for months. My daughter revealed a year later that she felt terribly guilty that she prayed her brother would die. She was neglected that whole

of her last year of high school. She couldn't deal with the grief in the house. She'd leave and go out with her friends. It wasn't until many years later when she became a mother that she had any perspective on what we were going through in losing our son. And I had little perspective on what she was going through because I was so wrapped up in trying to keep Patrick alive.

Gretchen

Both Gretchen and Tom saw the effects of the guilt their surviving children carried for years.

Young children don't know that wishing won't make it so. In fact, some religions teach that bad thoughts are tantamount to bad deeds. Children often wish their parents and siblings were dead. First of all, they really don't know what dead is. When children say they wish someone were dead, the translation is that they are angry, maybe very angry. It is not uncommon for a child to wish his competitor dead (translation, banished). It is even more common to wish a sick brother dead because of all the time and attention that brother is absorbing. If you wish your brother dead and he dies, the guilt can be a powerful force. Since young children don't make the clear distinction between fantasy and reality, they sometimes feel that their wish has killed their brother. They are sure they are responsible. Carrying that guilt around for years can have adverse effects on the child.

The antidote that can avert the harmful effects is to bring those feelings out into the open so they can be put in perspective. The child needs to have permission to talk about feelings he is afraid may be unacceptable. He then needs to understand that he is not responsible for causing the tragedy. It would be wise for a parent to anticipate that a sibling may be harboring guilty feelings and to talk about how usual and normal those feelings are.

Abandonment

Gretchen's story addresses the guilt and the abandonment themes we noted were common in children's reactions to the death of a sibling. Gretchen tells how her daughter felt so guilty about wishing her brother dead. She had that wish as a response to her profound feelings of having been abandoned. This teenage daughter was surrounded by grief for her entire senior year in high school. Her parents were so absorbed in her brother's catastrophic illness that she was virtually abandoned emotionally. Imagine what a child goes through during the illness of a brother or sister. The daily routine is inevitably disrupted as the parents are involved in treatment routines. Parents are less available, sometimes making it necessary for the child to assume extra responsibility. The sick sibling gets special privileges. Home life is changed; activities are restricted; friends can't come over to visit; meals may be catch-as-catch-can affairs; finances often become strained. They miss the companionship, even the conflict, with their ill sibling.

When a child has a lengthy illness, and then dies, the sibling may take on the role of comforting the parents, of being protective of their feelings, and of assuming added responsibilities. The atypical circumstances make these children different from their peers and, in so doing, subtly change the course of their development. That difference can have short-term consequences, or longer-term effects by veering the children's paths toward greater compassion or, conversely, toward a sense of having been cheated or deprived.

Harriet S. Schiff, in her helpful book *The Bereaved Parent,* describes her own experience following the death of her son.

> One of the most difficult roles for a mother or father, when a child dies, is to continue being a parent to surviving offspring. . . . Unfortunately, many surviving children suffer because their parents were unable to fulfill this responsibility, and the effects of their inability can be lifelong. . . . Six years later, our son, who was twelve when his brother died, remembers feeling unloved and alone during the entire grieving period and indeed for several years thereafter.

Parents have a hard time attending to the needs of grieving children when they are in the depths of their own grief. The children inevitably suffer. How much they suffer, how quickly the problems are resolved, how readily the family can do that vital work of grieving and regroup, are all functions of the overall health of the family unit.

Loss of Innocence

A third general theme we found was that children who lose their siblings also seem to lose a measure of their youthful innocence. They become much more aware of their own mortality than other children their age. They come to know, prematurely, that children are not invulnerable. They see grief firsthand. They feel the weight of their parents' compromised parental ability. They feel the weight of being an only child, or a remaining child, with all that implies.

One mother said that, after visiting the cemetery with her, her son asked if he would be put in a box, too, and if she would come and visit him when he was in the ground. Another mother said that her teenage daughters don't have the sense of invulnerability that is so characteristic of adolescents. Unlike their peers, they are fully aware that children do die. They have been robbed of that wonderfully carefree time, having eaten of the fruit of the tree of knowledge too early in life.

The vulnerabilities left by their premature experience with death can color children's choices years later. Josie said her two older daughters were watching as a speeding car swerved and hit their sister. That was some ten years ago.

> It's always in the back of their minds. Melissa is twenty and hates to drive. She'll ask a friend to drive or take the bus rather than drive a long distance herself. Bertha, on the other hand, doesn't mind driving long distances on highways, but she hates to drive around town. She always complains that there's too many people walking around. She can't stand to drive where there are pedestrians. You can't tell me they don't have scars.

Fallout

Patrice saw scars of a different nature in one of her surviving sons. She recalled an incident when her son was in the yard many months later and found a ball that belonged to his deceased brother. He happily gave it to his mother, thinking it might cheer her. Instead, Patrice said:

> I became a basket case. When my husband saw me so distraught, he yelled at my son. I cried. My son didn't know what hit him. He went into a shell. I noticed that he was becoming withdrawn and uncommunicative. I got worried about him. We decided to go into therapy as a family after he started to develop headaches, maybe two years after Sid's death. I think we all learned that it was okay for me to cry and for them to cry. My son realized that it was okay to talk about Sid and that it was okay if it made us sad. We learned that we could talk. A lot was accomplished.

In Patrice's case, long-range scars were averted by acknowledging a problem and attending to it. Cass had a very different experience.

> My mother lost a child when I was three. She never worked out her grief. When she was in her late eighties, fifty years after the death of her child, she was still talking about it. She had had twins and one of them died. She dressed me and my sister as twins. You don't have to be Freud! It colored my entire childhood, being dressed like a twin. On my sister's birthday, my mother grieved for the twin she lost and couldn't celebrate the surviving twin's birthday. My sister still has a lot of trouble with her birthday.

No one in Cass's family even acknowledged that a problem existed and, as a result, it festered, leaving scars and lifelong consequences.

Rachel said her teenage son felt it a particularly unwanted burden now to be an only son. His brother had been such a star and a take-charge person that he comfortably took a backseat. Now all the responsibility of being an only child sat heavily on his shoulders. He thought about being the focus of his parents' attention, about having to achieve, about being their primary source of pride, about giving his parents grandchildren some day, of knowing there was no one but him to look after them in their old age. All this was true. There was no way his parents could ease that burden for him. It helped that they saw the weight he was bearing and had the strength to wrap him in cotton-wool. They showered him with attention, resisted any temptation to lean on him, and indulged the few remaining years of his childhood.

One father had fewer resources and found himself looking to the surviving child for affirmation:

> After Ted killed himself, I felt monstrous. I kept thinking I was a terrible father. I did one thing wrong after another. Now I look to Josh. If his life isn't successful, then I'm a monster. He is my report card. I'm in the depths of despair if his life isn't going well.
>
> *Harry*

Josh has a heavy burden to bear, being the "report card" for his father. Harry remains too vulnerable to provide the parental protection even his grown son needs.

It's hard to know how much protection is right, enough, or too much. Harriet S. Schiff writes:

> Because of my protective instinct as a mother, I made a massive error in judgment at the funeral. I would not allow my son, aged twelve, to view the body of his dead brother because of the horror I felt seeing it. Difficult though it would have been, he should not have been denied this right. Unfortunately, no one told me I would do harm to my son with my protectiveness. And harm him it did because it took many years for him to lay his brother's ghost to rest.
>
> My daughter, then four, did not attend the funeral and

therefore had even less grasp of her brother's death. She is resentful even after all these years that she was cheated of the experience.

What to Expect

We see that children go through their own hell when illness and death enter the home. John Lavigne, who works with families following the death of a child from cancer, sees some of the problems that develop. He says that it is not uncommon for brothers or sisters to show signs of physical illness including complaints that mimic the symptoms of their deceased sibling. In addition, they sometimes have other physical symptoms, some of which last for an extended period of time, like headaches, bed-wetting, stomachaches, and the like. Problems with separation are not uncommon, such as fear of going to school or sleeping over at the home of a friend. Some children are so preoccupied that they can't concentrate adequately in school. All kinds of anxieties may emerge, including fear of doctors and hospitals, fear of dying, or any number of seemingly unrelated phobias.

Since guilty feelings often go unexpressed, they are likely to be seen in disguised form. The provocative behavior we mentioned earlier may be a symptom of hidden guilt. Symptoms that something is amiss include emotional withdrawal, decline in school grades, verbal and physical aggression, fears, and a variety of medical problems.

Some tips may help to avoid problems before they begin or to ameliorate problems once they are noticed. Children are often forgotten mourners. It is a lifesaver if a loving relative or family friend helps to provide parenting for the surviving children. Taking them on special outings, away from the grieving house, can help. Being around and offering a soft shoulder or sympathetic ear are vital services. A word that lets them know you understand how disrupted their life has been will go a long way.

Children need to be included in the family's mourning rituals. They fare better after the death if they have been included in the caregiving of a sick sibling. Moderation is the key. No child needs to be assigned caretaking responsibilities or to relieve over-burdened parents. If the child has been appropriately included, some of the guilt feelings may be short-circuited. Schiff cautions that excluding her children from the rituals did the opposite of what she intended; though her intent was to protect her children from pain, the unexpected result was that the children felt left out.

As Patrice said, it was essential for her son to learn that crying is okay. Children don't understand the flood of emotion around them. They need to have explanations geared to their age. They can be frightened by the outpouring of intense feelings and need comforting. Distractions are welcome. Children can bear the tears of their parents if they are being held, loved, protected, and includ-ed. Essentially, they need what the adults need, uncritical accep-tance, support, and understanding.

Since guilt is so prevalent in surviving children, it may help to anticipate it and put the topic on the table for discussion. It could be helpful to make up a story about another child who had all these guilty feelings haunting him like a ghost, or about a puppy who wished his brother dead, if that is more appropriate to the child's age. Telling stories about feelings you expect the child might have gives the child permission to experience the feelings. The stories tell the child that you are not angry or hurt, that you understand, that you are accepting, that the feelings belong to oth-ers as well. In short, it makes the feelings seem normal and okay. Then, eventually, the child can come to terms with her feelings and begin to heal.

The death of a sibling becomes a part of that child's history that he will carry forever. Some children bear the scars of feeling abandoned by their parents, of guilty feelings they've never come to resolve, of learning too soon that life can be tragic. But the same children can also learn a lesson of compassion and family solidarity. The loss leaves imprints both hurtful and enhancing. Those imprints need not be damaging in the long term if the child is warmly nurtured throughout the ordeal and the healing that follows.

Altered Relationships with Surviving Children

With the wisdom of hindsight, parents see, years later, the change in the course of their relationships with their surviving children. Some see that bonds with their surviving children became stretched and interrupted; others see bonds strengthened. Some see how overprotective they became; others see the opposite, a kind of fatalism that says they couldn't protect their children no matter what they did. Some mark mistakes they made. Just as rivers find new courses after a flood, so, too, do relationships.

Felicia's story

Amy had something very special. Even her nursery school teachers said the other kids went right to her. She had so much confidence. I gave her all this. I waited three years before I had Beth so Amy could have time with just me. I was gonna give her the world. I thought I could protect her from everything.

Beth was nine months old when Amy died. I feel bad that I don't remember when Beth started to walk. I don't remember those first two years. I see pictures and I say to myself, "Gee, she was really cute." All I remember is throwing her in the crib when she was crying and yelling at her, "Stop the screaming. You don't know what is going on." I just took care of Beth physically and even that was a challenge. You know that part where you connect with a baby; it's been hard to let her in.

I've been in therapy. I went to talk to someone about the lack of feelings I was having for Beth. I still have it. I couldn't open my heart; I have, but I haven't. If I could have changed the one who died, I would have, in a second. That's not easy to deal with. It's gotten better, but . . . I wouldn't change them now but it's taken me a long time to be able to say that and mean it.

I have no hopes for Beth. You know, with the first you

have all those hopes and dreams about what they'll be. Just the feeling you have inside for what they'll be like. I don't have that for Beth. That was taken with Amy.

I put so much of myself into Amy. I made sure she knew she was wonderful. Beth was colicky, a very hard baby. After a few months, things were just clicking with Beth. Mom and the two daughters were becoming a family. Beth adored Amy and followed her around in the walker. Then, before I really got to enjoy Beth, Amy died.

I used to curl Amy's hair every morning. All of her outfits matched, the socks, the ribbons; I was involved in that stuff. She'd always look perfect. With Beth, I just sort of let her go, which might not be so bad, but . . . I didn't have the heart for it with Beth. It wasn't important. I mean, who cares if you have on blue socks and a red ribbon; it isn't going to make any difference in your life really. You're forced to learn what matters and what doesn't. The soul is missing. It just went.

Felicia's story is told for the richness of the lessons it imparts to both bereaved parents and to members of the helping professions. Her story pointedly underscores the intended message of this book, that grief never has an ending, but rather involves a long-range process of integrating the effects of the trauma into the manner of living life. Felicia and Beth had, and still have, years of work to repair the hurt that was done by that sudden interruption of their early bonding. Bereaved parents should find in Felicia's story the assurance that all feelings are allowable and the knowledge that those feelings are repairable. They should banish guilt for even the most unspeakable of thoughts. They need to recognize that the most unacceptable of feelings heal if they can be acknowledged in an accepting, sympathetic climate. Parents must also know that some relationships are altered permanently and that they need to accept imperfection with good grace.

To those helpers among us, the family, the friends, and the mental health professionals, Felicia's lesson cries, "Don't you dare tell me that my grief should be over by now! My grief robbed me of watching Beth learn to walk. It robbed me of the delight of her first words. It robbed me of an intensely joyous bond that I may never come to feel." Perhaps, Felicia's passionate bond with her firstborn would have, in later years, proven to be too much. Teens often shun highly involved parents. Perhaps, being less concerned with ribbons and bows and letting Beth just "go" will give the child independence and backbone. Who knows? The important point is that the effects of grief, once the storm of grieving has subsided, will color, for better and worse, the rest of our lives.

Felicia was not alone in feeling that the glowing specialness of the firstborn was missing with the second child.

> The baby was a stranger to me. I didn't know her the same way I knew Douglas. Initially, I resented that it was Douglas who died and not her because he was my first. I had a lot more bond with Douglas. She was eleven months old when he died and it took a long time to be able to get to know her.
>
> *Denise*

The death of the cherished firstborn leaves a unique slot vacant. It seems as if the blush of first love becomes tarnished, changing everything that follows. One can't help but be reminded of the allegory of the expulsion from the Garden of Eden.

If death tarnishes some of the idealism of a family, it also enhances an idealism of a different sort. Quite a number of parents say that they hold the values of family cohesiveness tighter ever since the death. Maintaining the closeness becomes paramount; protecting the family relationships becomes a guiding principle.

> My son is seriously dating a woman of a different religion and this would have bothered me a great deal. But I've learned something from Sheila's death. There is nothing that either of my children could do that would make me risk our relationship. I can't risk losing another child. So I am much more accepting of his choice than I would have been.
>
> *Charles*

> I think I never appreciated my children before Tanya died.
> I took them for granted. Now I cherish them.
>
> *Veronica*

> Before I wasn't as careful about what I said to Otto. Now
> I have to be careful with him. I know how important it is to
> have a good relationship with him.
>
> *Evelyn*

In a dozen different ways, parents said they changed the way they perceived and the way they related to their surviving children. And many noted that a similar awakening took place in their older children. Several said the children were extra attentive to their needs, called a little more often, visited more often, and gave those small kindnesses that said they wanted to provide what pleasure and comfort they could.

Overprotection

Another way in which parents evidence the heightened value of surviving children and their feelings of vulnerability is to become overprotective. One mother who lost her child suddenly to an illness said she became a hypochondriac and remains that way almost a decade later. Terror overtakes her at the first fever, and she sees catastrophe where none is likely.

> Life is fragile. My healthiest, most robust child died. I
> used to be a bit anxious. Now I'm an extreme magnifica-
> tion of what I was in matters of health—mine, my husband's,
> and the kids'. I don't want the kids to see the world as a
> dangerous place. My two older boys do. My six-year-old is
> not affected.
>
> *Rhoda*

A father commented that his daughter looked at him with exasperation and said, "Do you know that you said, 'Be careful' twenty-three times." Parents who lose children in accidents have a devil of a time when their other children travel those same paths. While some children can take the overprotection in stride, others rebel. Whereas one of Patrice's sons understands his mother's need to keep tabs on him, another son feels constricted by her vigilance.

> I became overprotective. That has lasted to today. I won't let my youngest go off by himself on his bike. My oldest son is twenty-six and just moved out on his own. He was always considerate and would call me if he was going to be home late. My second son resented that he had to report to me. He moved out before he was twenty.

In Chapter 4 we saw the death of a child lead to overprotection in some parents and to fatalism in others.

> I'm defeated. It's not going to matter what I do. There is nothing I can do. I can't protect my children. I can't stop what's going to happen. I truly believed I could protect Amy. I lived in a bubble. Now I know you have no control over life.
>
> *Felicia*

Like Felicia, Josie developed a philosophy that protected her from suffering the same anxieties that Patrice and Rhoda experienced.

> I used to worry more. Now I realize that there are so many things I can't control. I can't sit around worrying. I didn't become overprotective. I give them a lot of freedom. I realize that I can't be God. Instead, Ginny watches over the family. Right now my daughter is on a bus to Canada. Ginny is watching out for that bus. My other daughter will be going on vacation to Italy. When she flies, I know I have an angel in heaven who watches over her.

Similarly, Patrice obtains comfort from knowing that the family has a special protector.

Sid is closer to me than my living sons because he's inside me and knows my every thought. I ask him every day to watch over his brothers. He's in higher authority. The other children pray to him.

The strategy works to keep them from constant worry.

Parents look back at the way they related to their surviving children during their intense grief and the later healing years. Not all like the picture they see.

A number of parents see conflict with their surviving children in those early days that could have been avoided if they had the wisdom of hindsight. It is only that hindsight and the healing of time that have allowed them to mend the fences of those embattled relationships.

> After Lauren died, I needed Sharon so much I was probably choking her. I needed her all the time because I needed to know she was alive. She couldn't handle it. A friend helped me to back off eventually. I realized I couldn't call her and see her all the time. I needed to give her room, but I needed the constant reaffirmation that she was still there.
>
> *Sandra*

In Sandra's case, the terror she experienced following Lauren's death led her to put her surviving daughter in a stranglehold. In turn, Sharon reacted by struggling to break free in the best way she knew how, by running fast and far. In every family, the grief of one member ripples through the unit and creates reactions in each other member.

> I threw up terribly strong opposition to my daughter getting married. We argued about it and I said a lot of things I regret. She was determined to go ahead with the wedding and threatened to have it without me. I woke up and realized that I couldn't face having a wedding if Hank wasn't going to be there. That wedding was the biggest and scariest thing I had to face. Once I came to terms with what I was

feeling, I knew that the last thing I wanted to do was alienate the only child I had left.

Pauline

With similar hindsight, Betty looked inside her heart and got to the core of her conflict with her surviving daughter. The two of them "fought, and yelled, and screamed" at each other through the storm of their grief. In the midst of one fight, her daughter accused, "Tom was your favorite and you wish that I had died instead of him." With great courage, Betty said she did some heavy soul-searching and knew that, for a fleeting moment, she had felt that and that her daughter had seen it. Once the words were out in the open, the two could begin to talk and come to terms. The mending took a long time. Betty knew a milestone had been passed when her daughter named her first child Tom. As Betty spoke of those deep wounds, I was reminded of the poignant story *The Thorn Birds* in which the cherished son dies, leaving the daughter and mother to mend their damaged link. This, too, is part of the family's work of grieving.

My relationship with my daughter changed dramatically after Dick died. We had been very close. We were able to talk about anything. Now there's a wall between us and I have to be careful not to offend her. I think that she was jealous of the grief I had for so long after Dick died. We were at a wedding about a year later and I filled with tears. I overheard her say that it was about time I got over it. She couldn't stand that I was still grieving.

Louise

We know that the weed of resentment comes to full bloom in the right soil and climate. The depth of emotion following a loss does tend to nurture buried resentments. But we also know that the weed doesn't take root and flourish if there is no seed. I listened for those seeds as the interview with Louise continued. In talking about funeral observances, Louise mentioned that she'd made a mistake, years previously, when her husband died, in not allowing her young daughter to attend, thinking that she was being protective. She noted that her daughter mourned deeply for her father and resented her mother for not allowing her to have that last good-bye. Louise remarried and said that her daughter grieved so for her father that she never allowed herself to get close to her stepfather. More resentment. Years later, Louise divorced her second husband. Again, her daughter resented the years the family lived in turmoil through her mother's troubled second marriage. The seeds of resentment were waiting for a fertile climate. When Dick died, the many accumulated resentments flourished. Relationships are unlikely to self-destruct following a loss unless there is some foreshadowing.

Subsequent Children

The passage of time does not erase the history of the family. It adds to it. Integrating that history into the fiber of daily life is one of the important tasks of mourning. Surviving children have been an integral part of the crisis in the family and are an ongoing part of the process of grief-work. They, like the parents, have been weaving that identifying information into their lives throughout the illness and mourning. In a sense, they are up to speed. As subsequent children are born, they, too, must be brought up to speed and taught the history of the family. The subsequent children in all the families we interviewed were fully aware that they had a sibling who died. Josie's subsequent children have been taught to say their prayers asking God to protect their family and their sister who is in heaven. Even as small children, they drew family pictures including Ginny floating in the sky.

Like Josie, Patrice keeps Sid's memory green these fourteen years after his death. Her children all know that she goes to the cemetery to care for their brother's grave and how meaningful that time is to her.

> I go to the cemetery often. I used to go every week, but now I go about every other week in the winter. It's my quiet time to spend with Sid. I prefer to go alone. I put flowers on

his grave and clean it and keep it neat. It's the only way I
have to still take care of him.

Every home I entered for the interviews had pictures of the
child they lost prominently displayed. That history adorned the
walls and tabletops for all to see. The newest family members have
that family record; it is as natural a part of their environment as
the kitchen table. They comfortably learn about the part their
deceased sibling played in the family's dance.

The birth of a child subsequent to the loss can be an awakening if the timing is right. One couple had another child ten
months after their loss and found the birth restoring. But when
Patrice thought she was pregnant two years after Sid died, she said:

> I was beside myself thinking that I had betrayed my son.
> Sid was my baby and I wanted him to stay the baby. I didn't
> want another child. But four years later when I got pregnant
> with Will, I was very happy. I got paranoid that something
> would be wrong with this baby and was a lunatic for a long
> time. But Will is a sheer delight. I'd sit by his crib and wait
> for him to wake up in the morning. He's a sweet child.
> When Will did a family tree in kindergarten, he put Sid and
> a dog off to the side.

When Stephanie became pregnant without planning, she realized that her due date was the anniversary of Jesse's death. She said
that as the date approached she was in a frenzy, hoping the child
would not be born on that exact date. She got to the day, prayed
to make it through the day, and went gratefully to bed when the
day ended. She awakened at 3 A.M. when her membrane ruptured.
Her daughter was born the following day. She said that she is
determined to put the most positive twist on that twist of fate by
telling her daughter that she is the "gift of healing."

Felicia's son, born four years after Amy died, is another child
who became a healing gift.

> It was Beth who kept us alive and Ben who brought us
> back. He's not connected to Amy. Beth will always be

Amyandbeth; they were a team. But Ben is just Ben. I see him so differently. Ben is now going through the fresh stage and trying my patience. But when Beth went through it, I assumed that it was because Amy was gone. I couldn't stand what she was doing and I couldn't stand her. With Ben, I realize that it is just his age.

For better or worse, the subsequent child is less connected with memories of the loss and of the deceased child. You can't look in your mind's eye and see him playing with the child you lost. They didn't bathe together or compete over toys. In our interviews, we didn't run across an instance where the subsequent child did not revitalize the family. However, that must be qualified by saying that the event was not without significant pain. Many parents, less innocent or naive than they had been, are more frightened, knowing full well what can happen. Some feel depleted and wonder if they will have the wherewithal to cope with the demands of a newborn. A few feel guilty giving their love to a new child. As we have noted, any joy brings a twinge of sadness with it.

The option to reawaken through a new life is closed for those beyond the childbearing years. For me, the birth of my first grandchild three years after my son died became a true awakening. The pleasure I felt in holding her when she was just an hour old was the first real pleasure I had experienced since the day he was diagnosed. The timing was right. I was at a point where I could let my heart open, and open it did. That little girl is joy unencumbered, a fresh breeze breathing life back into my soul.

Children born subsequent to the loss of a child often bring new life both literally and figuratively. How well these children fare emotionally depends on the manner in which they are woven into that family. Problems can develop if the new child is expected to fill the void left by the deceased child. Each child must create a position of his own and not fit into one that was occupied by someone else. Since lost children are often idealized, no subsequent child can live up to the image of "the most loving," or "the most talented" as his brother was. Real children spill milk and drive their parents to distraction. Deceased children don't do these things but may become saints, perfect and obedient.

Children may not feel valued for themselves and suffer with problems of self-esteem if they perceive that they were wanted to fill a vacated role. Physical resemblance or personality resemblance, real or imagined, can color the way in which parents relate to subsequent children. The resemblance may be positive or negative. In either case, the parent is carrying baggage into the relationship that has the potential to warp. That possibility, of course, exists when there has been no loss. The parent who views her newborn as the Olympian she never got to be is potentially headed for problems. The bereaved family has the built-in possibility of falling into the trap of unconsciously trying to replace the lost child and therefore expecting the subsequent child to walk in shoes that don't fit.

Parents who have an overwhelming preference for a child of the same sex as the deceased may be skirting the abyss of trying to replace the lost child. Denise imagined herself raising a brood of boys ever since she could remember. Her firstborn was the son she dreamed of having. She saw the daughter she had three years later as a playmate for her son.

> I realized that my daughter was a stranger to me. I didn't really know her; I related to her through Douglas. I resented that it was Douglas who died and not her because he was a boy and my first.

After Douglas died, Denise had trouble learning to relate to this little girl. When she got pregnant, she said she never once entertained the notion that this child would not be a boy. It was shocking to learn, a month before the birth, that her new baby would be a girl. Denise is the mother of girls. To the extent that she grieves for her dreams, and grieves for the son she had so briefly, she and her daughters are encumbered with that excess baggage. She is forced to relate to who they are not, instead of who they are.

Replacement Children

Josie was quite clear in her own mind that she wanted to have another child after Ginny was killed. But she recalls that so many of her friends and family had the idea that she was replacing Ginny. In her mind, she was having another child, not another Ginny.

> I really wanted more children, but my husband kept saying, "Well, maybe." After Ginny died he wanted another baby too. Then we had Morgan and I said, "Grief makes you crazy." We went ahead and had two more kids. One wasn't enough! It gave me back that time with little kids again that would have been gone.
>
> People would say to me, "I hope you have a boy because if you have a girl you'll think that baby is Ginny." And I thought, "What, are you nuts? There's no way I would think that another baby of mine would be Ginny." Some people would say to me, "Aren't you going to name her Ginny?" And I looked at them and I said, "No. I have a Ginny and she's in heaven. This one will be Sharon." I was so thrilled it was another girl. I like the dresses and all that cute stuff. I wanted another girl and they would have preferred that I had a boy. People say the weirdest things.

Josie never entertained the idea of replacing Ginny. She enjoyed children and the "cute stuff." She found herself bemused, if not annoyed, when friends would intimate that this new child would somehow replace the child she lost.

Gretchen was less clear about what she wanted. While she initially thought she wanted to have additional children to recapture a sense of family, she soon found that her motives were mixed.

> Two years after Patrick died, my husband and I decided to adopt two children from Yugoslavia. We went through all the red tape and made the arrangements. The children were in

an orphanage and we went there to pick them up. We got there and all the time we were there I kept saying to myself that I really didn't want this. But we brought the children home. They were such nice children. My husband wanted them. But my life didn't go back to the way it was before Pat died. That little boy wasn't Pat. I thought these children would make us a family again.

When I began to see that these children didn't give me Patrick back, I went into a deep depression and was hospitalized. Luckily, the adoption agency was able to find a wonderful family in the next town who wanted the children. I couldn't keep them. I had been in such deep denial. I was turning back the clock instead of moving ahead and trying to make a life for myself.

Gretchen

Any attempt to turn the clock back is doomed. A child born subsequent to the loss of an older child can be either an attempt to move forward or backward. What we term "replacement child" is any child conceived in an attempt to avoid dealing with the grief over the loss. That's not always a clear distinction. Gretchen's case is pretty clear. She was trying to replace a child and a lifestyle she lost. The attempt backfired. In other instances, the replacement child lives in the shadow of the lost sibling. Comparisons are made. The child is forced into shoes that don't fit. The parent fails to see the child for who she is but rather sees her own wishes projected onto the child. Since no child is a blank screen to reflect another's image, conflict is inevitable. Having a subsequent child is a restoring event. Having a replacement child is an avoidance and, by definition, problematic. No one can successfully reoccupy a vacated role.

Trickle-Down

The phrase we psychologists sometimes use to describe this "trickle-down" effect is "the generational ooze." Although the phrase may be new, you've seen the system in operation. You're all too familiar with families in which three or more generations have problems with alcoholism. Children who are abused are at risk of becoming abusive parents of children, who, in turn, may become abusive. Society is struggling with the problem of how to stop the ooze when several generations of a family remain on welfare.

Patterns of thinking and behaving are taught to successive generations. There are consistent and identifiable personality characteristics associated with alcoholic families, with abusive families, and with chronic welfare families that become part of the heritage given to the next generation. The abused child is one who learns that her environment is not trustworthy. She learns that she is an object for the expression of someone else's rage or sexual desires; she learns to suppress or alter her feelings so she can tolerate the intolerable. These warps become part of her personality development and get taught to her children. The case of abuse is an extreme; it is an example of how a problem in one generation gets transmitted to subsequent generations.

The death of a child knocks parents out of the parental box to some degree and for some length of time. To some extent, the parents' ability to fill their functions as parents is compromised. As in the extremes of parental alcoholism, parental abuse, and in some chronic welfare families, there is a situation of compromised parental adequacy. Parental inadequacy leaves identifiable scars that have some degree of impact on the child's development and personality formation. The extent and duration of these effects are a function of the developmental stage of the child, the length and severity of the deprivation, and the adequacy of the parent-substitute(s).

Grieving parents are often out of the parental box for a relatively brief period compared, for example, to chronically abusive or alcoholic parents. Of course, older children may fare better with parental absence than younger ones. Everybody will be better off if there is a kindly aunt to pick up the slack for as long as is needed. Without a parent-substitute, young children, left without adequate emotional support for lengthy periods of time, are likely to have scars.

To see the generational ooze in effect, let's take a look at Jack's story. It is the story of an exaggeration of the theme of overprotection that we've seen is a not uncommon by-product of the loss of a child. The story demonstrates the transmission of the effects of mourning to subsequent generations. It provides a pointed example of the phenomenon of "trickle-down."

Jack's story

A man I shall call Jack consulted me about marital and social problems he was having. He described himself as being very bland, just like his father. Jack sees his father as a man who appears to have an emotional wall around him. Looking back, Jack noted that his father was virtually forced into distancing himself emotionally because his mother, Jack's grandmother, was so smothering and overprotective. It emerged, as we talked, that Jack's father, Dominick, was a "replacement child," conceived to replace a seven-year-old who was killed in an accident.

Dominick's mother appeared obsessed with safety, keeping her surviving children and new son close to her apron strings and issuing frequent and impassioned reminders of the perils of the world. The persistence and pervasiveness of this tendency of the mother to paint the world as a threatening, dangerous place had reverse effects on Dominick and his older sister, who experienced first-hand the death of her brother and the family grief. The sister and her daughter, these many years later, retain lives dominated by fear, perceiving the world outside the immediate security of the family nest as potentially hostile.

In contrast to his sister and her daughter, Dominick and his son, Jack, are both risk-takers. Jack heard family lore about his father as a child climbing on roofs and engaging in numerous dangerous activities that threw his mother and sister into terror. Jack developed early as a risk-taker, scuba diving untrained prior to the allowable age for certification, and going on to become a wreck and cave diver, pushing the limits of time and depth.

The family history, as related by this man, spoke volumes about the long-term consequences of the death of a child. The reactions to the bereaved mother's overprotectiveness had opposite effects on sister and brother, which oozed down to the third generation.

The sister reacted to her mother's fearfulness by becoming fearful and carrying those fears, like an infection, into the next generation. Grandmother, mother, and daughter all saw the world as dangerous, with unknown perils hiding in each corner. The pervasive sense of vulnerability was set in motion by a tragic accident. The grandmother's fearfulness infected the son in an equal and opposite fashion. He defied all terror, stared it in the face, and took unreasonable risks. In psychology, we call that behavior "counterphobic," meaning that a person engages repeatedly in behavior he most fears. Father infected son. The story is a dramatic illustration of the manner in which mourning alters the shape of a family and how that new shape contours later generations.

When "Special" Children Die

We have noted that each person in a family has a unique position that contributes to the distinctive dance pattern of that family. A child who deviates from the norm in any way creates a role that has greater power to sculpt the interactions of the family unit than the role filled by the middle-of-the road child. For instance, a child who can play the violin at age four may set the parents' focus on the nurturance of that talent, affecting family priorities, time and money expenditure, apportionment of attention and praise, and so forth. Similarly, a child with chronic physical or mental health problems commands more than an equal share of family resources.

Among the families we interviewed, several had children with cystic fibrosis; several children were handicapped with varying degrees of mental retardation; two suffered from schizophrenia; several were addicted to drugs and behaving antisocially. The common denominator among these diverse families is that a compelling problem shaped the family interaction. The family is set apart because it is different, by its own and by outsiders' definitions.

Children don't like to be different. The child with red hair, the very tall one, the one who wears glasses becomes known by those distinguishing marks. Certainly, a child with physical or mental problems stands out and will influence the way in which the family goes about its business and the way other families relate to it. The child with a brother who suffers from schizophrenia may be colored by the "odd" behavior of his sibling. The well children often have great ambivalence about a sibling who brands the family.

A family must mold itself to special demands. The child with cystic fibrosis requires continual and intensive treatment, absorbing time, energy, money, and concern. Well siblings are drawn into the vortex with profound consequences that shape values and relationships both positively and negatively.

The family lives under the cloud created by the knowledge that children with cystic fibrosis often die young. We have seen that a certain amount of preparedness before the death of a child allows for anticipatory grief and the beginnings of the process of integrating the loss even prior to the death. Anticipatory grief appears not to have occurred with the cystic fibrosis families in this study. Grief didn't begin because: the period of anticipation is too lengthy; the family readily denied the inevitability of an early demise because there are periods of improved health; the illness and treatment became a way of life and not a preparation for separation. The illness saps the resources of the family and diminishes its ability to cope. Families of children with cystic fibrosis seem to suffer profoundly following the child's death partly because family life revolved around the illness.

So much of one mother's self-definition became "caregiver" that, after the death of her daughter from cystic fibrosis, she volunteered to work caring for babies with AIDS. She continues that work ten years later.

Another mother whose son died following years of suffering with cystic fibrosis said her surviving children told her:

> You spent so much time worrying about him when he was alive, we were afraid that there would be nothing left for us after he died.

Many siblings of chronically ill children live with the effects of having their parents' resources drained by the illness. Their grief is often accompanied by ambivalence.

But ambivalence is not the reaction of the parents when their special children die. The parents bond to special-needs children in a very unique and intense way as they minister to the exceptional demands. Insofar as the lives of parents of retarded children, schizophrenic children, and chronically ill children are defined by those illnesses, the parents are the more bereft following the loss. Parents of handicapped children adapt their dreams for the future to include permanent caregiving. They resemble unprepared empty-nesters when the dependent child dies. Their lives are deprived of meaning and purpose in a singular and profound manner.

Anna and her husband, now in their retirement years, knew that they would always have to look after Peter, who had been diagnosed as schizophrenic in his adolescence. He lived in their home. It was difficult for them to go out for any period of time because there was no one to care for Peter. Vacations were out of the question. They saved any discretionary money they might have spent for entertainment to build a nest egg for Peter's care after their death. Peter's illness colored virtually every aspect of their lives.

> Now I don't have to worry about Peter anymore. We were putting money aside in case his brother had to take care of him. There's a hole left by not having to worry about what's going to become of him. We were still taking care of him. The focus of our lives was always on Peter, the saving, the planning, the things we could and couldn't hope to do. It was something we knew we'd always have to do. Peter was withdrawn and when he was home, he was in his room. So now I try to think of him as there, in his favorite, safe place.
>
> *Anna*

Peter, though suffering from schizophrenia, was highly intelligent, a gifted writer, and "a nice young man," to quote his mother. Missing him was less ambivalent than it is for the families of children who are not "nice," according to their parents' values.

Sherry's family had to contend with the conflicted emotions of grief and relief. Her son Jason's aberrant behavior shaped the lives of each family member during his life and after his death.

Life was torture while Jason was alive. He started drinking when he was in college. He was into drugs and in trouble with the police. He was a criminal; he stole things. He flirted with danger all the time. He got all the attention in the family. The fact that he was so bad had a profound influence on the other children. His younger brother chose to go to Annapolis to bring some pride back into the family. When Jason was killed, I had a moment of relief. He was finally safe. Maybe he would not have shaped up his life. Then the pain got so bad I thought I was losing my mind.

Sherry

The antisocial behavior of a family member creates havoc, dividing a family against itself. Drug treatment programs require family participation and often siblings resent being "sentenced" to treatment when they have done nothing wrong. The family is shamed and the conforming children tainted. Parents ride the roller-coaster of hope and despair. Sherry, Jason's mother, told of her roller-coaster; Matt, his father, tells of his.

The day before he died, Jason did a big catering job. I think he was starting to come around. He was a troubled kid and there was a feeling of relief when he died. You know, what if he didn't turn around? Then there's the guilt of feeling relieved. But I do think he was beginning to come around. He could have made something of his life.

Despite the torment of life with a deviant child, hope for rehabilitation remains. The parents are no less devastated than parents of conforming children when that child dies. Then begins the process of mending the damage done to the family by the divisiveness that the deviant behavior created. Note the reaction of Jason's brother who went to a military academy to "bring some pride back into the family." That mending has far-reaching consequences. The sculpture that was the form and shape of that family now takes on entirely new dimensions.

The long-range consequences following the death of a child with special needs may be even more pervasive than for healthy children. That may be so because the bent of the family has been contorted to fit the shape of the problem. The vacated role had that much more of a profound influence on the way the family ordered itself. Values, priorities, allocation of resources, all shift dramatically. We saw many instances in which these families continued to struggle many years later with the process of coming to terms with the loss of special children.

Grandparents

The grandparent generation has been called "the forgotten mourners." Their grief is complicated by their knowledge that they have lived a life, raised a family, and accomplished some of their goals in contrast to the grandchild, who has been deprived of his chance at life. A father told me that his father kept saying that he's old and that it should have been him who died. Grandparents grieve for the cherished grandchild. They additionally grieve for the pain their child is going through.

> My parents hurt so much seeing me sad. They needed for me to be back the way I was. I had to back away from them for more than a year. They didn't want to hear how I sounded. They couldn't stand my grief. What was the point of talking to them if I had to put on a show? They hurt too much to be any help to me at all.
>
> *Margot*

Just as the parents' marriages became turbulent in the early aftermath, so too did the marriages of grandparents.

> My father got angry with God and my mother turned toward religion and prays a lot, looking for an answer. It

affected their marriage a lot. My father says, "I'll see her sooner than you." I think it has changed the way he feels about dying.

Felicia

The death of a child reverberates throughout the family system, coloring every relationship.

The family is much like the mobile that used to hang over your child's crib. Both the family and the mobile just keep on turning, for such is the nature of time. The distinctive elements that make up the mobile sway and balance, blending into a harmonious whole. The interplay of the elements, coupled with the sway, make up the appeal of the mobile.

If any part of the mobile is removed, the unit no longer looks the same, nor does it turn or balance as it did. New parts can be added and attempts made to replace the missing piece. The repairs can be done artfully and with great care, but one truth is inescapable: It is no longer the same mobile and it never will be again.

It has been our observation that the death of a child leads irrevocably to philosophical changes in each of the individuals, as well as changes to the structure of the marital relationship and to the balance and sway of family interactions. Next we will look at the social milieu, at social support, and at the adaptations that take place in friendships and patterns of social interaction.

Chapter Seven

Social Relationships

> When people outside the immediate family are encoun-
> tered who do not allow . . . expressions of emotions and
> thoughts about deceased children, it creates a resentment that
> is difficult to control. Subsequently, the time comes when
> parents begin to separate themselves from insensitive and
> uncaring people in their environments who insist on keeping
> channels of communication closed.
>
> Many times a wedge is driven between those suffering the
> loss and very dear and close friends. We can refer to this as a
> "wedge of ignorance"—ignorance about the great impor-
> tance of open . . . communication.
>
> —Ronald J. Knapp, *Beyond Endurance*

After the loss of a child, individuals are transformed; their marriages evolve to a new level; family systems modify; and the
manner of relating to the outer circle beyond the family undergoes a myriad of adaptations. If parents are not the people they
used to be, if their wants and needs, their perceptions and values,
all change, it is inevitable that their behavior in social situations
will also change. Though the parents may appear the same to the
casual observer, they are different in the way they see, hear, and
feel. They, unavoidably, will react differently to what goes on
around them. Thus, a comment or an attitude that might have

passed unnoticed before the loss rings with a different timbre afterward.

The first half of this chapter is a potpourri that contains wisdom gathered from the interviews. It targets the people who make up the parents' immediate and extended support systems. It tells what they found valuable and what they found objectionable and why. It suggests approaches to caregivers that are most and least likely to be comforting.

In the second half of the chapter we investigate the changed social perspectives of the parents. We will see how their friendships evolve, how they handle themselves socially, how they manage the difficult times, and how that all comes together to allow reentry into the social milieu.

Social Support

An orphan is a child without a parent. A widow or widower is a person who has lost a spouse. As Enid said in Chapter 2, there is no word to identify to the outside world a parent who has lost a child. Perhaps the concept is too unthinkable. There are greater impediments to getting social support for bereaved parents than for other mourners. The biggest impediment is that other parents shy away from the living embodiment of their worst nightmare. If this nightmare happened to you, then it could happen to me. Besides not wanting to be reminded that such atrocities do happen, most people, even with the best of intentions, don't know what to say or do. Potential sources of support avoid the eerie and the awkward. Consequently, bereaved parents are often avoided and become victims of social ostracism. Some feel like lepers.

In addition to feeling isolated, many mothers say they feel judged, as if people are telling them how they should be grieving, comparing them with some imagined standard of the proper pace of progressing through grief. If they have a good day, friends jump to the conclusion that the grief is over; if they have a bad day, they need a shrink.

It's interesting that people judge you either way; either you're avoiding it or stuck in it. You can't win either way. I guess the death of a child is such a threat to others that they distance themselves by either judging you negatively or putting you on a pedestal.

Donna

I think Donna had it right. People try to make grief disappear because it's such a threat. The first threat is the vague feeling of contagion we already mentioned. A more benevolent explanation is that such rampant emotion makes the observer feel absolutely helpless. So they try to make it go away.

My wife put Jason's name on our Christmas cards and some friends said to us, "Get over it." We lost a child and he's dead. He didn't disappear. He's still part of our lives.

Matt

The friends who told Matt to "Get over it" were not protecting Matt; they were protecting themselves from the feelings of impotence and uselessness his continued grief aroused in them. In all likelihood, they were kind, well-intentioned people. They didn't know what to do for Matt, so it was easier to become impatient with him and tell him to stop arousing their sense of helplessness.

Another way of assuaging the sense of helplessness that is aroused by coming face-to-face with catastrophe is to hide behind ritual. That is a tactic often utilized by some clergy who are more at home with theology and liturgy than with people.

I spoke with a rabbi and told him that we had Thomas's remains cremated in Colorado where he was killed. He said, "Jews don't do that." I told him, "This Jew did," and hung up the phone. I have no use for the clergy since. All you get is judgment.

Betty

What Betty needed was some compassion. She needed a visit. She needed to find a way to make her decision to cremate her son's remains feel okay. She did not need to be dealt a guilt trip.

Both clergy and lay caregivers hide behind canned phrases when they have no idea what to say. It is easier to know what abrades than to know what soothes in those early months. Telling someone whose child has just died that there was some hidden purpose behind this tragedy with a statement like, "God works in mysterious ways," does not bring comfort. Reassurances that the "pain will get better," that "time heals," that "he's in a better place," that "you still have two other children," grate on the nerves of the bereaved and certainly do not console. All of the above statements negate what the parent is feeling at the moment, utter devastation and hopelessness. The parent needs to have that anguish acknowledged and accepted, not whitewashed. Mourners are frightened by the intensity of their pain and become more so when caregivers appear frightened. They need someone to be with them physically and emotionally with a stance that communicates, "I'll stick with you through this." The "time heals" cliché should be relegated to the scrap heap when it comes to trying to provide solace to the bereaved.

Honest comments such as, "I can't imagine what it must be like for you," signal that you're receptive to hear what it's like and open the door for communication. Silence, accompanied by a comforting gesture and a posture that indicates, "I'm listening," is helpful. There is no right thing to say. When a grief-stricken parent asks "Why?" he really doesn't expect a scholarly lecture. There is no answer. The only reasonable stance is to reiterate what the parent is feeling, that the death is unfair and wrong and a hideous tragedy.

The public seems to harbor some notion about the right time-frame for grieving. Pop psychology supports the notion of a year or two being about right, something like the directions to keep the turkey in the oven for about three hours. I think that the notion of a time limit is compelling for the caregivers because it gets them off the hook. A year is quite a lot of time to be listening with empathy, to be weighted down by the anguish of a loved one or to be on the giving side of a relationship that presumably once was two-sided. When a caregiver says, "You should be over this by now," she may also be saying, "I'm reaching the end of my caregiving rope."

> My sister told me that I'm not doing well. I told her that every day I drive over the George Washington Bridge on the way to work and I don't jump off. That's doing well!
>
> *Cass*

Her sister would have done better to ask if there was any way she could help or anything she should be doing. She would have done well to call and visit more often. She would have done well to extend compassion and hold judgment.

Help!

Professional Counselors

Many parents consult mental health professionals, social workers, psychologists, and psychiatrists. They do so because they feel they are unable to cope with the intensity of their emotions or because their relationships with spouses and surviving children are in turmoil or because they need someone to guide them through the tunnel. Many are also told by friends that they need professional help because they are not grieving correctly. In more than a few instances the professionals themselves confirm that the parents are grieving incorrectly by inferring that their grief should be further along than it is, or some such judgment. While many bereaved parents are substantially helped by their counseling, too many come away empty or, worse, feeling additionally criticized and isolated. Counselors must remain aware of their own difficulty in dealing with such a powerful subject and secondly be sensitive to the feelings of helplessness that accompany attempts to comfort the grieving.

Min called the hot line at St. Vincent's Hospital because she and her husband were "at each other's throats" during that first year.

Some young kid answered and he just couldn't relate. He didn't have a clue what I was talking about. He had never even had a child, so how could he possibly relate?

Regina went to a psychologist who, she said, didn't know what to do with her. He had no ability to help her with the grief, so he turned to something he was better equipped to handle. According to Regina, "All he wanted to do was talk about my divorce." Looking back, parents seem bemused by the ineptness of the counselors they consulted; in retrospect, they see that their counselors were often as bewildered as they and had just as few answers. The more helpful counselors acknowledged that they had little more than compassion and caring to offer in those early months. Therapists became valuable later in the grief-work when parents became aware that they were stuck or that they were having difficulties with family relationships. The work of therapy is to help people learn how to solve problems. There is no way to solve or fix that initial anguish. It has to run its course. There are ways to help people who get stuck or bogged down in guilt, for example.

A number of mothers sought counseling because they were in such pain they thought they were going crazy. They needed reassurance. Several were given medications to help with sleep disturbances and to alleviate depression. Rarely did those medications help either to make the parent feel better in the present or to shorten the grief process. Grief can't be sidetracked; it must be worked through.

Those who derive the most benefit from professional counseling are usually far enough beyond the initial stages to be able to focus and to learn from the process. Those with specific issues to be worked out are likely to profit most. In Chapter 6, we saw Felicia and Patrice, who availed themselves of professional counseling with very positive results. Felicia recognized that her grief was endangering her relationship with her surviving daughter. Patrice knew that her son's poor school performance was related to turmoil created by the way the family was coping with their loss. Both had very positive therapeutic experiences. Therapy helps with inner conflict and with troubled relationships. It helps when the mourner needs a nonjudgmental ear and the reassurance that her reactions are not crazy. It does not attenuate raw grief.

While in that early stage of grief that is characterized by chaotic emotions, the bereaved search, sometimes frantically, for lifelines, for hope, for anything to make the pain bearable.

> I read every book about grief because I thought I was losing my mind. It felt like I was insane; I was losing it; I couldn't concentrate.
>
> *Sherry*

Many read voluminously, seeking order, reassurance, hope; many go to clergy, to friends and family, to professional counselors, to self-help groups, and to psychics.

Support Groups:
The Bereaved Help the Bereaved

All the people in this study were, at one time, members of The Compassionate Friends (TCF). Furthermore, they remained in some contact with the group, through the newsletters or through friends, so that they learned about our request for volunteers many years past their loss. For obvious reasons, we were not able to interview those parents who went to a self-help group once, found it wanting, and never returned. Therefore, we have no information about people who didn't choose to seek that kind of help or those who found it didn't help at all. So when we say that people found more help from other bereaved parents than they did from assorted counselors, we are talking about a very select group of parents.

Other bereaved parents know better than to prescribe how grief should be or to suggest that it should be better by now. There is consolation in seeing other parents who lost children still standing upright, dressing neatly, going about their daily routines, and even having the strength to comfort others. There is reassurance in knowing that everyone else in the room feels the same despair and manages to function through it.

In the six years following Jules's suicide, Theda made a new life for herself. She ended a hurtful marriage; she completed a graduate degree; she became active in her new profession; yet she felt lonely and isolated in her grief.

> My sister found the address of the national headquarters of TCF in Illinois. I wrote to them and they sent me names of five other people in my geographic area who were bereaved parents. I decided to start a self-help group. I put a notice in the newspaper for people who had lost a child. I got all those people together and started the TCF chapter. It was like finding water in the desert after all those years of wandering and wondering if I was going crazy.
>
> *Theda*

The solace that TCF members find is alleviation of the feeling of being alone. TCF is a refuge where the full impact of what these parents have experienced is understood and shared. The members are an island of souls who have been or still are in hell, but who have to function in the real world among foreigners who don't know the language of the island.

> I am the co-leader of the county TCF chapter and I write the newsletter. That newsletter is my main dedication to my daughter. I devour the newsletters I receive from all over the country. I can relate to what they say. I don't feel so alone. I'm isolated in the world outside of TCF. Everything outside of TCF is the outside world; they don't really know me. The outside expects you to be better in a year or so. By this point, eight years later, everybody expects you to be better. At TCF you can have tears in your eyes and not apologize.
>
> *Veronica*

While the group provides refuge, it is a refuge no one would volunteer to enter.

> I hated to be part of that group [TCF]. They were all parents who lost children. I didn't want my son's name to be

put on the list among dead children. But I kept going back. I didn't talk for six months. It took so long. I never knew it took so long. You think you're going out of your mind. I didn't want to survive. Part of me is dead. But part of me came back to life.

Min

Finding a refuge, relief from isolation, and people who speak the same language are a few of the benefits of self-help groups. Like Alcoholics Anonymous and other such groups, twenty-four-hour support is available.

One night, about three months after Kevin died, I found myself walking alone from room to room yelling, "I want my baby back!" I screamed from about 11 to 1 A.M. I thought I would lose my mind. I called Stephanie [the TCF chapter leader] in the middle of the night. She said, "It's okay. I've seen this happen at about six months, but for you it's happening a little earlier." So when it happened again, I was more in control. I knew it would pass. It was a relief to be able to scream, to unload like that.

Regina

What was so therapeutic about Stephanie's response to Regina was the reassurance she gave that the craziness was pretty standard fare on this island. Outsiders too often lack that insight. Knowing that her rampage was not unusual, Regina became a little less frightened and a little more in charge during the raging storm.

Support Groups: The Downside

Lest I paint the picture that TCF or self-help groups are the last word in grief support, let me present the downside. Any group is only as helpful as the people who comprise it at the moment. TCF is a particularly fluid group with members coming for as few as one or two meetings or for many years. People come to meetings or skip meetings as needed. The fluidity and the continual entry of new members is a disruptive influence that dilutes the formation of intimate relationships. There is no continuity from one meeting to the next as there are in professionally led therapy groups. That factor assures that the group remains superficial. It is, as the name implies, a support group, not a therapy group.

The leaders are self-selected from among the membership and have no formal training in leadership or in any of the mental health disciplines. So if one member dominates the group or a newcomer is too reticent to speak up, no trained leader is there to address the problem. Therapy groups that have professional leaders with educational backgrounds in the social sciences and in group dynamics provide better safety for the members. Professional leaders are better able to identify, manage, and control potentially problematic interactions and to keep the group moving in a mentally healthy direction.

For example, one of the leaders of the TCF group called me, knowing that I was both a member of the group and a trained psychologist, and expressed concern about the possible hurtfulness of some of the policies of another of the leaders. She questioned whether the other leader may have been leading the group in an unhealthy or unproductive direction. A self-help group has to muddle through these dilemmas on its own. It gets very little direction from the national organization; and the national organization itself is run by people without specific training or education in the helping professions. At times it seems akin to asking someone who has never taken a course in anatomy to please remove your appendix. It can be a case of the blind leading the blind.

As with all groups, problems arise with internal and external political issues, with rivalries among members or leaders, and with power concerns. Here are some impressions of a father who led a chapter for several years.

> I learned in TCF that if you were compassionate before your child died, you became more kindly. If you were a selfish SOB, then you acted as if you were the only one who lost a child. I finally got angry and quit the chapter. People

competed. One parent would say, "My child died in an accident and I never got to say good-bye to him. At least you got
to say good-bye." Or someone whose child had a lengthy illness might say to someone whose child died in an accident,
"My child suffered; at least yours didn't suffer." I couldn't
stand the one-up-man-ship. I had to leave.

Thomas

Another factor several parents mentioned as their reason for
ceasing attendance is that the continual presence of the newly
bereaved weighs too heavily as they begin to experience a lightening of their own grief. There comes a time to move on.

Quite a number of the leaders of TCF chapters are many
years past their loss, some a decade or more past. Though one
purpose of this book is to raise awareness of the fact that bereaved
parents never get over their grief, parents do reinvest in life and
gradually spend less time actively focused on grief. I have some
questions about what motivates people to remain intimately
involved with grief for more than a decade. One TCF leader con-
fided in me that she had concerns about another leader who
worked tirelessly in her responsibilities to the chapter, who continued to introduce herself and sign her writings as "Clara's
Mom," and who reliably attended all the special TCF programs
more than a decade after her loss. Her concern was that this
mother may be a poor role model for the newly bereaved, being
an example of unremitting grief that spans decades. Without
knowing the mother better, I could not guess what her continued dedication to TCF represented, healthy resolution or
unhealthy preoccupation.

There are many varied motives for parents to remain active in a
support group for a long period of time. Some motives suggest
positive resolution of grief, movement forward, investment in
meaningful, altruistic pursuits. Some motives suggest a retreat. The
group may provide a place to hide or a place to hold on to the
past. Self-help groups have leaders who represent both ends of
the continuum and therefore can create an environment either
conducive to growth or to stagnation.

Social Support: Some Dos and Don'ts

There are many more women than men in TCF. We noted in the chapter on marriages how men and women, in general, tend to grieve differently. The same sex-role conditioning that equips men and women to deal with mourning differently sets them up to have different needs and expectations from the people around them. Traditional sex-role training allows women to be more needy and dependent. A woman can be powerless without looking weak. She can admit problems and request help without being seen in a negative light. Secondly, women are acculturated to express feelings, confide in friends, and have intimacy with others.

A man's social conditioning encourages casual relationships, playing feelings close to the vest, and keeping his own counsel. Appearing strong and in control is more highly socially valued for men than for women. While a woman can yield to the open expression of grief and still appear female, the man who does so may risk, or fear risking, appearing less masculine. After a couple has lost a child, it is common in this society to hear people ask the husband how his wife is doing. The social expectation is that he will not only to be in control of his own emotions but will also be in a position to provide comfort to his bereaved wife!

> I was dragged by my wife to the first TCF meeting two months after Tommy died. There were nineteen women and one other man. If not for him, I would have left. My wife dropped out after a while, but for the next five years I never missed a meeting. At almost every meeting someone would ask me, "How's Mona doing?" They never asked how I was.
>
> *Thomas*

Thomas represents a substantial minority of men, those who have the "pursuer" personality style we described in Chapter 5, the type of personality that moves toward others. However, the majority of men may go about the grief-work by closing down emotionally, by returning to work quickly and with a vengeance, by becoming caregivers for their wives and surviving children, and by staying tightly in control. Men can work out emotions through physical activity, hard labor, or aggressive play. Women go about the grief-work more within a social context. Women can express their emotions with less risk of losing face than a man might feel; they don't have to contort themselves to appear other than they are. It is more socially acceptable for women to ask for support and lean on others than it is for men.

For Caregivers

Talking is comforting. Talking is comprehending. Talking is healing. Talking is remembering. This parents must do. This they will do. Anyone standing between these parents and their need to express themselves about the experience of their loss and their feelings relative to it will be deeply resented, and eventually their friendship discarded or pushed aside.

—Ronald J. Knapp, *Beyond Endurance*

Here we report some of the perceptions of the parents about friends who were more or less helpful during the early grief. Given that mourners are, by definition, emotionally drained, it is often difficult for them to find the strength to ask for what they need. In addition, grief is a time of such emotional chaos that it seems impossible for the mourners even to know what they need, no less ask for it. By a process of trial and error, mourners discover what feels supportive and what hurts. The do's and the don'ts become readily apparent.

The "do's":

My friends didn't know what to do for us. They told me later that they went to the library and asked for books on grief so they could learn more about what might be helpful. They allowed me to talk and to cry. They just sat with me day in and day out. I'd do anything for them now.

Felicia

Our friends were a tremendous help. I don't know how I would have gotten through without them. But not only our friends helped. It seemed like people in the community we didn't even know came to do what they could. I'd get home and find a casserole on the doorstep. You can't imagine how that helped me get through, just to know that some anonymous person cared enough to go out of her way to do something kind for us. Besides, I couldn't have gotten food on the table no matter what.

Josie

The "don'ts":

My best friend and I had kids the same ages. They all grew up together. She hasn't set foot in my house since the day Jason died.

Sherry

Many of the parents we interviewed told similar stories. A sister, a best friend, or a member of the clergy stayed with them almost continually during the initial period. Talk wasn't necessary. Presence was vital. Those caregivers just sat, respected the need for the mourner to cry or not to cry, to scream and rail, to hide in sleep or to be whatever they needed to be during that agonizing and chaotic early period.

In the weeks and months following the funeral, help of a physical nature is welcome: cooking, cleaning, driving car pools, running errands. Keeping the daily routine going in some semblance of normalcy is comforting and leaves the mourner to do the work of mourning. Mom doesn't have to feel guilty that the house is in disarray or that the children don't have clean underwear or hot food.

The children need attention. It is too easy for caregivers to concentrate on the obviously bereaved parents and to overlook the small, silent mourners. The children need to be given the opportunity to participate in their special activities, to see friends, and to be among people who are not grieving. They especially need someone to acknowledge that they, too, are grieving and to offer them comfort and the opportunity to talk. It is awkward for children, just as it is for adults, to have friends who don't know what to say to them. They, too, are navigating a desert island, feeling different, tainted, and isolated.

In the words of one young teen:

> Going back to school after the death of your brother or sister is a hard thing to go through. At first there are three groups of people to deal with: people who give you a lot of support, people who don't know what to say and those who give you weird looks and stay away from you. This lasts for a little while.
>
> After a short time, changes with each group occur. Those who didn't know what to say start to speak to you. The group who kept away stops ignoring you. The people who gave you a lot of support slowly return to their own affairs. After about a month and a half, everything goes back to normal and is over to everyone except you. This is very difficult to accept and makes you feel all the more alone.
>
> After a long while, the shock for you goes away and it is then that you need the support from your friends, peers, and teachers. This month is the first anniversary of the death of my brother. Most people have forgotten and everything is right with the world. But it is not! Certainly not for my family and me.
>
> *Author Unknown*
> TCF Newsletter

Emotional support is vital. That often comes in a quiet form. Being present, listening, is usually more valuable than any words. Frequent telephone calls help. The offer of some distraction should be made with sensitivity to readiness. If you suggest an outing, respect whatever response is forthcoming. Caregivers are at their best if they follow the lead of the mourner. As anyone who has visited a house of mourning knows, moods shift rapidly. Crying, laughing, idle chat, warm reminiscences follow each other with no predictability. Never was the admonition to "go with the flow" more appropriate.

As the need for casseroles and car pools diminishes, be that a month or a year, other kinds of support become necessary. There are differences in the kinds of support that are needed during the active grieving period and the kinds of supportive remembrances bereaved parents need forever after.

> Our society has perpetrated a fraud. We are led to believe that the last thing bereaved parents would want to do is talk about the death of their child. The complete reverse is true. Parents want to talk and want someone to listen. Someone who can hear the crying of their soul . . .
> —Katherine F. Donnelly, *Recovering from the Loss of a Child*

After the first year, caregivers fade out of that role and back into the usual social intercourse with their friend. To do that is a disservice to friendship. The bereaved parent is not the same person who was your friend before the loss. She has been through a wringer and come out shaped subtly differently. Forever after, there will be a gaping wound in her soul that becomes inflamed on holidays, anniversaries, and for no reason that is apparent.

Not only anniversaries and holidays need to be acknowledged. All special occasions do. Weddings, graduations, and family celebrations are all times when bereaved parents remember and feel sad. Sensitive friends do a kindness when they tactfully acknowledge that, "This must be a tough day," and give the parent the opportunity to respond. Everyone we interviewed cherished a friend who would note, "Bobby would be graduating this year." We must caution that the people we interviewed constituted a unique subset of bereaved parents, notably those who find talking comforting. Others may respond differently and it behooves the caregiver to be sensitive to the response and guide themselves accordingly.

Patrice let her family know that she needed Sid to be remembered. So when her brother's daughter got married, the bride and groom honored Sid's memory by putting a scroll on each table that read:

In lieu of wedding favors we have made a donation to the Make-a-Wish Foundation. We are hopeful that the magic of this day can be shared with those who are less fortunate.

As a continuing memorial, Patrice's brother sends money to Boys' Town and the Leukemia Society in Sid's name every anniversary.

You can rest assured that the majority of bereaved mothers want to talk about their child. The same may be less true for fathers. Mothers want to reminisce; they want to hear their child's name; they want the empty place in their hearts to be acknowledged. The need to acknowledge the child's life and talk about him is almost universal. When one mother called to arrange for an interview for this research, I asked her what motivated her to participate. She said that now that it is six years since her daughter's death, few people talk about her daughter. The interview, she said, would give her the opportunity to talk about her, to reminisce, and to have someone who understood listen.

For the rest of their lives bereaved parents need to talk about the deceased child, to have birthdays and anniversaries remembered with calls, cards, and donations. Every bereaved parent we spoke with treasured a loved one who acknowledged the anniversary of the death. Too many well-meaning friends don't mention the day for fear of bringing back bad memories. As if any parent could forget the day their child died! The most kindly support comes from remembering and noting the date with some word or gesture of acknowledgment. "How are you today?" works fine.

> My best friend called every day for a year. She still remembers to call on every anniversary and special occasion. You can't imagine how good it is to know that someone is out there who cares enough to remember.
>
> *Wanda*

For Parents

It would be remiss to suggest that the whole burden of providing support rests with family and friends. The mourners must find it within themselves to let people know what they need. Many parents in our interview group found ways to reach for the support they craved.

The onus to initiate the reminiscences is not solely on the caregiver/friend. The bereaved parents themselves have to be more open in the communication of their wishes.

> Friends and family didn't know what to do for us. It was hard on them. I didn't know how to tell them at the time because I didn't know what I needed. I know now that it was our responsibility to make them at ease.
>
> *Gretchen*

Several of the people we interviewed indicated that they knew they had to teach their family and friends what they needed.

> I had to educate old friends how to deal with me. They stopped inviting me. You know, we were all pregnant about the same time and did all the birthday and holiday stuff together. But after the initial three months when everybody called up, I didn't hear from them. They stopped calling and inviting me. I asked one friend and she said, "We were going to invite you to so and so's communion, but we thought it would be hard on you." So finally, the second or third time someone said that to me, I said, "Do me a favor; invite me and I'll let you know if I'm up to it."
>
> My friends thought it was kind of peculiar that I would want to be around all their kids. But I wanted to see the kids because maybe they would share a memory with me. That was so important to me. I always talk about Kevin and I need new stories all the time. After that, word got around and I was invited.
>
> *Regina*

Regina was able to get the kind of treatment she needed because she told everyone. Karen had a different, but equally effective method of getting her needs met.

Nobody called me for a long time. I wrote to all my old friends and that opening freed them up to call me.

Assertive parents find the inner resources to tell their loved ones what gives them comfort. Parents who are less assertive believe that their friends should know how to help without being told. They stall out in resentment at how poorly they are treated. They remark about the failure of family to meet their needs and about the insensitive comments that are made to them. Their inability to recognize how bewildered and inept relatives feel leaves them more isolated. To mourners who find they fit into the shoe just described, the best recommendation is: If you are angry at people for giving too little, you probably haven't asked for enough. If you need people to behave differently, tell them how.

Like Regina, Patrice educated her family about her needs. No one knew how to handle the anniversary of her son's death. She asked her parents, her brother, and her best friend to meet her at the cemetery to talk about their memories of her son. She suggested that afterward they all go back to her mother's house for dinner. That memorial has become a tradition that has helped her immeasurably to find a way to keep the memory of her son alive and to spend a difficult day in the bosom of warm family.

Enid said that one of her brothers still, ten years after the death of her only child, buys her something on Mother's Day.

That floors me. It's so incredible that he has that sensitivity. He's wonderful. Each of my brothers sends me a note on the anniversary. They never forget.

Filtering Friendships

Bereaved parents sometimes find that over time their relationships have gone through a process of filtration. There are two major filters that I shall call "loyalty" and "genuineness." Loyal friends and family stick with the mourners despite their own discomfort, feelings of helplessness, and fear. Others fall by the wayside. In years to come, those who remain loyal come to be valued and cherished. Those who keep themselves at a distance become relegated to a position of polite acquaintance, if that.

It is often people who care deeply who cannot find the right words and defer making the condolence call. The procrastination may extend days, to weeks, to months until the sense of shame at not having called mounts and further hampers any approaches to the telephone. Meanwhile, the bereaved family is additionally bereft of much-needed sources of support. Too often the silence may be taken for indifference and the relationship teeters on the brink of extinction. The scenario is all too common. After the acute mourning has passed, the family may find itself with a substantially altered circle of friends.

> I'm not bothered by people who said stupid things. I'm bothered by friends and family who disappeared.
>
> *Alan*

The second filter, "genuineness," is a quality that is the opposite of pettiness and pretentiousness. Bereaved parents come to a deepening of values, a sense that time is too short to spend on inconsequential matters. Many of the interviewees said that they no longer have any tolerance for trivia. It becomes difficult to be sympathetic to someone who takes a small social slight seriously. They find that people who are, in their words, "whiners," arouse their annoyance. Losing a child lets people know without a doubt what is and is not important in life.

> I don't suffer fools lightly. I can't stand people who go crazy if the blue in the carpet doesn't match the blue in the drapes.
>
> *Cass*

> As far as friends go, they've completely changed. A lot of people I don't even associate with anymore. It has less to do with them than it does to do with how my outlook on life is totally different. The friends I used to have still have the

old outlook. What is important to them isn't to me anymore. As far as going out and doing things, I'd just as soon be home spending time with my kids. You need to take time and savor it with your family. We've made friends with other people who have lost children, some from TCF.

Barry

Most of our circle of friends has changed from before Joel's death. Some of them were mainly concerned with image and material things. That grates on my nerves. I'd like to tell them to stop whining. We're more selective now. We want to associate with people who are genuine, down-to-earth, and not pretentious. We've made friends with some of the people from TCF who think the way we do. We have one particular lasting relationship from when we were involved in TCF.

Rhoda

More than a few bereaved parents affirm what Rhoda said, that their circle of friends changed. They filter out, emotionally, at least, those people who were insensitive and absent. They filter out those whose values appear shallow or who seem to lack perspective.

The Hardest Question

In the beginning of a new relationship, one of the early getting-to-know-you questions often is, "How many children do you have?" What a dilemma that question poses for the newly bereaved. Do you include the deceased child? How can you exclude him? Do you make some explanation? That would certainly be a conversation stopper. Do you want to open yourself to this acquaintance or retain your privacy? Learning to answer that question is part of the grief-work, part of learning how to cope with life without your child. Response to that question often goes through several evolu-

tions as healing progresses. In the beginning when the loss constitutes the whole of your existence, there is no holding back. But as
time goes on, a selectivity comes about, and a style of response
emerges.

In the early months, fear of being asked that question made me
avoid social situations where there were people I didn't know.
Over time, I've developed a way to handle the question. If I can
anticipate the question, I can be prepared and mentally plan a
response. However, on one occasion, I was totally unprepared. As
a psychologist I was giving expert testimony in a custody case.
The attorney was reviewing my credentials, asking questions
about my education and training, a standard line of inquiry during which I had my guard down, cruising through the routine.
Then he asked, "How many children do you have, Dr.
Bernstein?" The question threw me out of balance and I hesitat-
ed so long that the attorney jabbed somewhat sarcastically, "Is that
a difficult question, Doctor?" He could not have known how very
difficult a question it was, so much so that I was at a loss to come
up with an answer.

Margot's explanation of how she has come, over the years, to
respond, is fairly typical.

How I answer depends. Sometimes I say, "I have my son."
When it feels safe, when I think it's someone I care enough
to share something personal with, then I tell them. It may
happen in the first meeting if I feel you're a person I have
this immediate connection with. If it's somebody I will
never see again in my life, that's fine. Then I just say, "I have
my son" and leave it at that.

One time, not long after Marion died, I met a woman
and she asked me the question and I told her that my daughter died in a car accident. And she had the nerve to insinu-
ate that my daughter must have been on something. So I
decided then and there that I would spare myself the awful
pain of having to hear that kind of nonsense.

But for a long time I felt guilty. I felt I was denying
Marion's life if I didn't include her. And sometimes that's

still a factor. My friends at TCF and I have come to the conclusion that we don't have to tell everything about ourselves just because somebody asks. That's not a denial of our children. I don't have to be naked out there. They're not telling me anything that's private and personal about their lives, so I don't feel I have to tell them. I don't tell my business associates, not if they're not going to be involved in my life.

Margot

You can see in Margot's explanation that the way in which she responds to the question has evolved over time. You can also see how the question sets off internal shock waves. It raises guilt about including or excluding the deceased child. It raises nostalgia in that the parent needs to include the child. The question initiates an immediate evaluation of the asker. Is she sensitive enough to hear the answer? Is she going to be a person with whom I will have a continuing relationship? Should I risk telling her the truth and letting her into my private world? What's more the dilemma doesn't go away. It changes with the years. It does, however, get easier with practice. Margot suggests that she and her friends at TCF have developed a kind of informal formula that tells them how to respond in different social situations.

Masks

The most essential ingredient . . . in surviving well . . . is to speak of the dead child unashamedly.

Harriet S. Schiff, *The Bereaved Parent*

When a bereaved parent speaks publicly about her deceased child, she is too often met with embarrassed silence. The listener may rapidly change the subject, not knowing how to respond. Rather than endure that awkwardness, many parents say they put on a mask of social propriety, park their grief/luggage at the door, and put on a happy face. The guise is contrived both for public consumption and as an exercise of whistling in the dark, to escape from the crushing weight for brief periods.

> I don't want to wallow in sadness. No one knows how I feel. Sometimes I feel guilty for that. I continue to carry on like a nut. I let it all out at night when no one is around and can see.
>
> *Shirley*

Brenda became a master of disguise. She says she never mentions Paul anymore, not to her surviving children, not to her family, not to her friends. She has erected a wall around her pain. The wall serves two vital functions. First, it protects her from the revival of acute grief, the descent into uncontrollable tears, whenever she thinks of her son. Secondly, she presents a social mask since it is apparent to any mourner that the life span of social support is limited. No one wants to be with a friend who is perpetually and openly grieving.

Brenda changed jobs some time after Paul's death. To all outward appearances she was a vibrant, cheerful, energetic member of the workforce. One day, two years later, a song was playing on the office radio that had been a favorite of Paul's. Unable to maintain the wall, her inner tears spilled through the mask. A co-worker asked her what was the matter. She revealed, for the first time in that environment, that she had lost a son. Though this scenario may represent an extreme case, it is not an uncommon phenomenon among bereaved parents.

> I feel that when you lose a child it makes you different from other people. It's like being maimed in a way. It doesn't show on the outside; but it still makes you different from other people. I've learned to keep it inside and not let it show on the outside. Nobody can really help you with it.
>
> *Sandra*

One of the TCF chapter leaders notes, "There are two Veronicas, one with the mask who goes to work and leads an active social life, and the unmasked Veronica who finds the only people to whom she can relate openly are the friends at TCF."

Rachel describes her pain as luggage she carries everywhere. She maintains the ability to put it down as she enters a room, but always knows where it is and that she will pick it up again as she moves on. Mourners become adept at parking their luggage, at playing Pagliacci, laughing on the outside while crying on the inside. When a friend says to a bereaved parent, "It's good to see you're back to yourself again," the parent sometimes feels a mildly bemused sense of betrayal. The friend is seeing what she wants to see, what makes her comfortable to see; the friend sees only the mask. Numerous parents echo the sentiment, "I am not the person I used to be. That person died with my child." There is a disservice to bereaved parents in failing to recognize that the luggage is always just outside the door.

Shirley reiterated the Pagliacci motif.

> I act the same, crazy. Close friends see me as a bit more serious, but basically the same. The reality is that everything is different. It's as if a line was drawn the day Alison was killed. Now there's no more of anything to look forward to. Alison will not be coming home for Christmas or Thanksgiving. There won't be any grandchildren. Sure, from day to day I look the same, act the same, laugh the same, but everything is different.
>
> *Shirley*

> The truth is that this life sucks most of the time. I keep asking, "Why me?" Even six years later I feel how much I miss her, how much we've been ripped off. It's unfair. How I wish I could hear her voice and all that stuff that the rest of the world just doesn't want to hear. Even her father [from whom Margot is divorced] who loved her and was a wonderful father—in a bad moment I called him because I thought I could share those feelings with him, stuff that nobody else wants to hear. He told me to stop pitying myself. I said, "Excuse me! You think that that's what this phone call is about, that I'm pitying myself?" And I knew he

was hurting; there was no question. So, I said, "I'll remember next time I need someone to listen, you won't be the person I call."

When I tell my [present] husband what I'm feeling, he really loves me and it bothers him to see me sad. It hasn't been easy for him. He tells me I should try to think about other things. I know how I have to be for him. I have to be without pain. I have to wear a mask for him. I certainly have to wear a mask for my parents. They need me to be the way I was. They can't stand to hear how sad I sound.

At work I have to be upbeat. Very few people even know I lost a daughter. The only ones who will listen are the other parents at TCF. They understand; they are wearing masks for the world too. A few of us who now lead the TCF meeting meet apart from the group where we have to be giving to the newly bereaved. We just talk among ourselves. We all talk about our children and our longing. All of us feel that death is no longer a threat to us. We laugh and cry and are ourselves without the pretense. I feel totally comfortable with them. I come home those nights feeling refreshed by just being able to take off the mask for a little while.

Margot

Margot so articulately recapitulates the sentiments of myriad bereaved parents; with their spouses, with their friends, with their extended family, with work associates, they put on the happy-face mask.

Handling Special Occasions

The worst days now are holidays: Thanksgiving, Christmas, Easter, Pentecost, birthdays, weddings, January 31—days meant as festivals of happiness and joy now are days of tears. The gap is too great between day and heart. Days of routine I can manage; no songs are expected. But how am I to sing in this desolate land, when there's always one too few?

—Nicholas Wolterstorff, *Lament for a Son*

After a couple of years, the bereaved family settles into new traditions regarding holidays. Changing things from how they used to be often helps to make the empty chair less prominent. Some families choose a change of venue, going to a sister's house instead of having Thanksgiving dinner at home, or using holiday time for vacationing away from home.

> That first Christmas after Sid died we decided to go away just to do something different. Some members of the family criticized that and said, "How could you do that?" I don't like people telling me what I should and should not be doing.
>
> *Patrice*

There are no rules governing grieving. Each individual and family have to work out their way to get through it. That process of finding a route that has the fewest emotional potholes is what constitutes the ongoing grief-work. The family needs to find routes for itself. Any attempts from outsiders to impose rules rankles. How can anyone recommend a detour around an obstacle if they have never been down that path? In any case, suggesting rules heaps guilt and doubt on the shoulders of people who truly don't need any.

Some families alter the Christmas routine. Most ultimately come back to old traditions, find deeper value for the togetherness of family holidays, and come to take renewed pleasure in the celebrations.

> The family looked to me for clues, like around Thanksgiving. My mother didn't want to have Thanksgiving around the house because everything was the first. A neighbor invited us over, the whole family, all of us. My mother, when she got the invitation, came directly to me and said, "What should we do?" I said, "Come on, let's go." In later years it was okay to go back to my mother's the way we always had.
>
> *Enid*

Though holiday celebrations are painful in the early years, they seem not to remain so for most families. While the backward glance at the empty chair never completely fades, the glance becomes more nostalgia and less anguish. Though recurring holidays evoke less pain in later years, special occasions still have the power to rekindle melancholy. The graduation of a deceased child's class often brings a resurgence of nostalgia even many years later. All life's landmarks, weddings, births, graduations, and such set off waves of sadness.

> If [my surviving daughter] gets promoted or when she gets married, all these things are going to have an edge to them that they didn't have before.
>
> —Katherine F. Donneley,
> *Recovering from the Loss*
> *of a Child*

Weddings have special power to evoke strong sentiment. As Charles put it:

> Now it's eighteen years later and I can't imagine attending my daughter's wedding without realizing that Sheila will never have a wedding.

Any wedding can be a threat to hard-earned equilibrium.

> Holidays and such are not particularly difficult for me, but the first wedding of one of her friends was very hard.
>
> *Michelle*

> I was very close with my sister before Tanya died. Her daughter was six months older than Tanya. Four years after Tanya's death, my niece was getting married. I couldn't go to her wedding. It was just too painful a reminder for me to face. I had to protect myself. My sister couldn't forgive me for not coming. The bride understood. But I'm alienated from my sister now. That's another loss. I want her in my life again.
>
> *Veronica*

The weddings of family members and of surviving children are often greeted with mixed emotions. The occasion can't help but be a poignant reminder. There is one child who will not be standing up as best man, one child who will not have a wedding of his own, one child whose offspring you will never hold.

Reentry

We took our first big plunge back into the world of enjoyment with a weekend trip four months after Robbie died. I felt like an unnatural mother, a heartless, unfeeling person who could consider having fun with her child newly dead.
—Harriet S. Schiff, *The Bereaved Parent*

Taking that plunge back into the world of enjoyment comes after differing lengths of time for different people. A major factor in how long it takes before a parent is able to resume social activities seems to be whether the death was sudden or anticipated. In the case of Schiff, above, her son ailed for many years with a heart condition. So, four months after his death, the long-encumbered family needed to revive and reconnect. So it was with Barbara and Charles, whose daughter fought a long battle against cancer.

Sheila died on November 14. We had a vacation planned for Christmas. I said that I thought we really had to get on with life. It was the best thing we could have done. It was tinged with sadness, but the other two had been neglected through the illness and they needed this. They have good memories of that vacation. It was fun. We needed to be together.

There is wide variability in the amount of time bereaved parents need before they can resume pleasurable activities. And the kinds of activities are carefully selected. Pleasure is a triple-edged sword. First, having fun evokes a measure of guilt, the feeling that it is unseemly to feel good after your child has died. Secondly, grief is a connection to the deceased child. As you relinquish grief, you also loosen the link with that child. The child becomes a little further from reach. Thirdly, pleasurable occasions trigger longing. The most wonderful occasion is occasion for missing the child who is no longer a part of the family festivity. Happiness is never again without longing. It is never again pure.

Returning to social activities is difficult for the bereaved for numerous reasons. Seeing other people casually enjoying life is in stark contrast to their internal heaviness. I recall going to a restaurant, hearing music and watching people dancing, feeling as if everyone else was made of feathers and I was made of lead. Other parents told me they feared going to church or public places where the sight of intact families with healthy children aroused such envy and longing.

There does come a time when parents find themselves laughing at a movie or they catch themselves once again tapping their feet to music; it happens without warning, usually as a surprise. The parent hears her own laughter and, at first, recoils. Gradually, with advances and regressions, the indomitable human spirit prevails. Pleasure becomes possible and okay.

Helpful Hints

Here are a few suggestions that may be helpful to friends and family who offer support to grieving families.

A LOVE SONG

The mention of my child's name may bring tears to my eyes—but it never fails to bring music to my ears.

If you really are my friend, please don't keep me from hearing the beautiful music. It soothes my broken heart and fills my soul with Love.

Nancy Williams
TCF Newsletter

1. Mention the child's name. It won't remind parents of their loss. They haven't forgotten!

2. Avoid the clichés that minimize the tragedy, statements like: "Your child is in a better place," or "You can always have another child," or "You'll feel better in time."
3. Cry with the mourners if you are so moved. It's empathic.
4. Gentle touches, warm embraces, and hands held are comforting gestures that replace words when there are no adequate words.
5. Accept the family's decisions, regardless of whether you agree.
6. Respect the time frame of each individual's grieving.
7. Give special attention to the siblings. They are grieving also and are frequently forgotten.
8. No one has to be strong for anyone else.
9. Expect any milestone, graduation, wedding, anniversary, holiday, or special occasion to evoke longing. Acknowledge that in the years to come.
10. Keep in touch. Call, write, or visit on special occasions forever after.

The following may be helpful to parents as they grapple with the social world:

1. Follow your own instincts. Only you can determine what is best for you at any given moment.
2. Be forthright and tell people what feels right for you.
3. Planning holidays and special occasions in advance and letting others know your wishes may ease the way.
4. Asking for help gives your loved ones a chance to feel useful.
5. Seek professional counseling if and when you have a sense that you need a hand to help you climb out of the pit.
6. Banish guilt; it has no value.
7. Allow pleasure.
8. Remember that your friends are probably wandering in uncharted waters too.
9. You are likely to go up and down the roller-coaster rapidly and without warning.
10. Be a living memorial to your child by being the best you can be, by enjoying life, and by making a difference.

Chapter Eight

Religion and Spirituality

> My confrontation with faith began that April day in 1985
> as I studied Christopher's stilled face. . . . I knew then there
> were only two possibilities—either this tragic world was all
> there was or there was something far greater beyond this life
> that I did not yet comprehend. . . . In these rare moments of
> extreme pain, we may sense, just for an instant, that some-
> thing does lie beyond the mists of this confining physical
> world in which we live.
>
> —John Bramblett, *When Good-Bye Is Forever*

Tough Questions

There is no religion I know that portrays its deity as capricious
or arbitrary. We don't see paintings in art museums depicting
God shooting dice with the lives of humankind. We are taught to
have faith in a god who infuses the world with goodness, order,
and virtue. But search though we may, there is no sense, no good,
no purpose, no virtue that we can fathom in the death of a child.
It is out of the order of the universe; it is wrong. Parents who lose
a child confront an incredible dilemma. How is it possible in a just
and godly world that evil survives and goodness dies?

I used to believe in God. But then I think that my son was
into environmental causes, that he lobbied for animal rights,

that he was an advocate for the homeless, that he fought to end racial injustice. Those were his visions, to have an impact on the ills of the world. I am left with no choice but to ask, "Why didn't Hitler die at twenty-three?"

Betty

If there is a God, I am still angry with Him. I was brought up to believe and not to question. But it doesn't make sense; your kids die, and lousy people live forever. How could God put you through this kind of pain? It just doesn't make sense.

Barry

The dilemma Betty and Barry confront is one that has engaged philosophers, authors, and sages throughout the ages. The problem they pose is how to continue to believe that God is just in the face of such an apparent contradiction. If religion teaches that God gives people what they deserve, and people who appear to be good suffer terribly, then it must be that the good people are not good after all. Some parents do indeed feel that they are being punished for some sin they unknowingly committed. It would be too unsettling were we to conclude that perhaps God made a mistake. To do so would shatter our basic security in the justice and predictability of the world. Life seems comfortably orderly when we can feel assured that good things happen to people who are good and that bad people get what they deserve.

Rabbi Harold Kushner, in *When Bad Things Happen to Good People,* explores the history of thinking about the question of why God allows bad things to happen to good people, adding his own wise interpretations. The book is recommended to those trying to unravel that knot. Kushner appears to question the neat answers other thinkers have come up with, wisely avoiding the temptation to find simple answers to complex questions. If healing is to be found, this rabbi counsels, it is not in finding the reason why we are struck, but in asking how we can move on from here.

In the face of any catastrophe that throws the world out of balance, people need desperately to restore equilibrium and reestablish their footing. Let's look at several of the strategies people use in their attempt to regain the security of knowing that the world is predictable and just.

Blaming the Victim

While religious scholars ponder the dilemma of God's apparent unfairness, psychologists look at the same problem from another angle. Psychologists see the disruption brought about when something bad happens to someone we thought to be good. The natural inclination is to preserve our belief in a tidy world where everyone gets his just desserts; so in trying to find a way to resolve the contradiction, we seek flaws in the victim. After all, finding the victim blameworthy is a psychologically safer course than questioning God's wisdom or acknowledging that the ground on which we walk is indeed shaky. If we find the victim to have been remiss, we know how to protect ourselves. If the world is topsy-turvy, we don't.

Listen to the line of questioning when a friend tells another that his neighbor was robbed. Did he keep the lights on when he went out? Why didn't he put in an alarm system? Did he have enough insurance? The hearer of such a tale of misfortune is thrown out of balance and needs to reestablish equilibrium. He does so by questioning the victim, to find out whether some folly or inadequacy of the victim's contributed to his misery. If he can find the victim at fault, he can feel safer, less vulnerable. Thus, religious philosophers and psychologists note the same phenomenon. When bad things happen, people tend to maintain their belief in a just world, in a fair God, and blame the victim. Blaming the victim allows us to continue to believe that God is just and the world is predictable.

However, the death of a child is one striking instance that defies the explanation that the victim may, somehow, have been at fault. That explanation is too far a stretch of the imagination. Since it is impossible to question the victim, no course is left for bereaved parents but to question their faith, question the wisdom of God, and question the justice of the world.

Minimizing

The next line of defense to which people resort in their attempt to maintain their psychological equilibrium upon hearing terrible news is to render the news less terrible. They need to cushion its impact. Making a calamity appear less so allows one to continue to believe that God is good and wouldn't arbitrarily rain anguish upon our heads. "He's in a better place." So goes the line of thinking that lets us keep faith. "She was such a lovely child that God wanted her for an angel," is a thought that has at its basis the need to neutralize an abhorrence. Yet, when well-wishers offer words about God wanting this beautiful child as an angel, parents envision a God turned selfish and jealous who would snatch this treasure for Himself. Though these words of comfort are frequently offered to mourners, they seldom bring comfort. Nor do most mourners find these hollow platitudes restore their faith.

> "Your child is happy with Jesus now." That has to be among the worst things anyone can say. I was brought up in the church and several family members are ministers. I attend regularly and am an active member. I think it's all baloney that you're supposed to find comfort in your religion. None of it meant anything in trying to find any way to make sense of this or to get comfort.
>
> *Loretta*

That is not to say that Loretta is any less an active member of her church these many years later than she was before her son died. She remains committed to her religion and to God. She is saying simply that her faith, strong and enduring as it is, brought no comfort in her grief.

Josie refused the notion that the God she revered had any hand in the death of her child.

> People say it's God's will. Oh, how I hate that. I say, no, no. I do not think that God picked her and said, "That car should

hit her." Maybe that kid speeding down the block was care-
less, but I don't believe God did that to my daughter.

Saying that the tragedy is God's will comes across as a white-
wash, a meaningless attempt to explain the inexplicable.

R a t i o n a l i z i n g

Another method of justifying our faith in the pervasive wisdom of
God is the frequently heard assertion that God doesn't give us
more than we can bear. Each instance of suicide is an instance of
a person who is dealt more than he can bear. There were many
instances in this study of parents whose lives disintegrated following the loss and who remain withdrawn and nonproductive
through a decade and more. A few spoke of lives so thrown off
track that they became a shadow of their former selves, derailed
and dysfunctional. God gave them more than they could bear and
they crumbled under the weight.

> My husband got withdrawn. He put a wall between us.
> He wouldn't talk. He got nasty. That wasn't like him. It got
> worse and worse, and he wound up quitting his job and
> going from one project to another. He was floundering. He
> went from being an accountant to working in a gas station.
> Then he took off to live with some monks in New Mexico.
> He's back now, still working one menial job after another,
> living under the same roof with me but totally estranged. We
> only talk if we need something. My family is destroyed.
>
> *Brenda*

God is given credit for bringing pain so that we might appreciate pleasure more. This is another rationalization, an example of
how we assure ourselves that the world is orderly, purposeful, and
not arbitrary. One parent said that he thought that simply wasn't a
fair trade. There could be no pleasure that was worth the agony he
experienced. This same father further questioned why he would
be singled out for this lesson when the rest of the world seemed

to be going about its pleasures without experiencing comparable torment.

Thus, the psychological defenses people employ to help them maintain their faith in a just world in the face of catastrophe often come crashing down for the bereaved parent. Faith is questioned. God's infinite wisdom is questioned. The rightness and fairness of the world are questioned.

No Answers

Religion brings few answers; it brings little diminution of pain. The God to whom parents had always turned for wisdom and serenity betrayed their trust. When Pauline heard the words from her priest, "Hank is with God," all she could feel was fury toward a God who would take her son.

> "Blessed are those who mourn for they will be comforted," is a cliché I had heard over and over in church. I never felt comforted. I didn't think I could survive the pain.
>
> *Cass*

A number of parents who were raised with strong ties to the church found themselves questioning. Many feel alienated, isolated, without solace. Brought up to believe that faith would bring consolation, they feel deserted in the hour of their greatest need.

For a few of the parents we interviewed, that loss of faith in formal religion persisted, to be replaced as the years progressed by a different kind of spirituality. Over time, they come to feel more strongly than ever the need to give succor wherever they are able. They truly know the value of people supporting people.

Rituals

Though it is not immediately apparent, and does not provide surcease from pain, religious ritual does indeed serve several very useful functions for the bereaved. At a time when emotions are thrown into chaos, the funeral rites provide structure. Rituals give direction during the initial state of disorganization and confusion when thinking or planning is out of the question. The funeral in each religion is a script, easily followed. It gives families something concrete to do, thereby adding a sense of control.

In addition to its function of giving structure and direction, ritual marks a formal rite of passage. Death is too easily denied; it is compelling to imagine that the child is merely off on a trip or away at camp. The process of the funeral, the viewing, if there is one, the presence of a casket, the burial or cremation, all serve to make the death real. Accepting the reality of the loss is one of the first tasks of the grief-work. It has to be acknowledged in order to begin the later tasks of integrating the loss.

One of the mothers we interviewed chose to have her daughter's body cremated out of state where her fatal accident occurred. She never attended any ceremony, never saw her daughter's body, never formally marked the death. For a very long time, she maintained the illusion that her daughter was still away on vacation. The lack of a ritual encumbered the healing process.

A third important function that formal services provide is to bring people together. The next of kin are the primary mourners, immediate family next, more distant family, friends, and casual acquaintances all attend and have a prescribed role in the script. Each person who comes adds support in some measure, directly or indirectly, doing a service or merely being present.

> I had some real revelations after Kenneth died. I saw the kindness of the people in the church. They were tremendously helpful. They made a luncheon before the funeral. They came out of the woodwork. They picked up relatives at the airport; they baby-sat; they listened; they visited. I didn't even know the people who brought food. They were exceptional. It reminded me of the Quaker saying, "Christ has no other hands than ours." I learned that you can't necessarily directly repay the people who were so helpful, but you can pass it along to someone else. That is the true meaning of the church in a crisis, the people, the community, not the ritual.
>
> *Loretta*

But it is the ritual that brings the community together in the first place and that is why it is so vital.

Clergy

The clergy are among the first to have contact with a family that has sustained a loss; they have a position of authority in the community; they are expected, by dint of their training and experience, to be knowledgeable; by tradition, they are seen as sources of consolation. All these conditions place great responsibility and great power in the hands of clerics. Despite the fact that ministering to the bereaved is an important function they serve in the community, seminary training in the psychology of bereavement is often cursory at best. Priests, ministers, and rabbis are no different from the rest of the community who find themselves at a loss for words in the face of profound grief. Feeling helpless is even worse for them because they know it is their responsibility to be helpful. In order to feel useful, they do what they know how to do best, preside over the formal ceremonies.

> It raised a lot of questions when I saw the ministers in my church were afraid to be with me. To see people I had admired distance themselves made me question religion. I began to think that maybe being a minister is just another job opportunity.
>
> *Donna*

Whether a family attends church or synagogue regularly or not at all, has deep religious convictions or virtually none, a member of the clergy is almost universally called upon to preside over the funeral rites in this society. Despite their ubiquitous presence, however, the clergy seems to provide more of a ceremonial than a psychological function. Parkes, Glick, and Weiss, in their book *The First Year of Bereavement,* found in their research with bereaved families that members of the clergy are rarely cited as sources of help. They officiate at the ceremonies, lend dignity to the proceedings, and furnish direction and structure. Their robed presence offers the serenity that comes with tradition and familiarity. However, they frequently lack the training or experience to know how to relate to grieving parishioners in a consoling way. Too often, their robes shield them; their rituals become walls behind which they retreat. The members of the clergy who were truly soothing to the parents we interviewed left their rites and robes behind, became members of the family, and let their humanity emerge.

Helpful Clergy

Bereaved parents are seldom looking for any words of wisdom. There simply are none that can provide any relief. There are no answers. There is no right way to grieve. Emotions don't come in "right" or "wrong." There are no words that can be said that will make this tragedy make sense. The greatest comfort comes from merely being with the bereaved physically and emotionally. That means listening without judgment and creating an atmosphere that gives permission for the parents to feel whatever they do at the moment. Allowing someone to express even the most outrageous feelings without negation is the vital gift of acceptance. Those members of the clergy, or the community at large, who try to impose order or reason will find themselves speaking to deaf ears. Religion cannot be imposed. Platitudes give offense. Wise clergy understand this. They know that the greatest comfort they can give newly bereaved parents is their accepting presence and their compassion.

> The comfort I derived was from the rabbi as a friend and not the rabbi in his rabbinical role. He didn't give religious explanations. He called daily for a year. He remembered the anniversary. That was incredibly meaningful and supportive.
>
> *Bruce*

> The priest was present at the hospital when my son was pronounced dead. I was so numb, like a puppet; I'd do what-

ever people told me to do. It got so bad that I had my suicide planned. But Father Gregory came every day and just
sat by my bed. Sometimes he didn't even say anything; he
was just there. He told me to call any time, day or night. He
became part of our family. It helped when he told me, "Look
to Mary, our Blessed Mother, for support, for she too lost a
son." I felt I wasn't singled out. Father Gregory was the most
beneficial person in turning my life around.

Patrice

Josie, a member of the same parish as Patrice, had a similarly
beneficial experience with Father Gregory. She said that her
daughter's breathing was maintained by a respirator for several
days after she was struck by a car. Father Gregory stayed at the
hospital during the long hours of waiting. He sat with the parents
as the doctors told them that the child would not recover. He was
with them when they made the decision to donate her organs. He
sat with them in the predawn hour when they held her and
allowed the respirator that artificially sustained her breathing to
be turned off. He made no judgments; he offered no counsel; he
had no words of solace to alleviate the pain. He merely stayed
with the parents, held their hands, accepted their decisions, and
gave his warmth. Josie says that, without a doubt, his support
throughout the following year gave her the strength to survive
and the will to heal. He remains, these many years later, close with
the family, visits regularly, and always remembers the anniversary
with a call or visit.

Unhelpful Clergy

My own experience with our rabbi could not have been more different from the experiences of Josie and Patrice. Rabbi Goldstein
knew our family for many years, having taught each of our three
children, now in their twenties, for their Bar and Bat Mitzvahs. He
called my son one Friday to ask him to come to synagogue that
night so they would have a minyan (the required quorum of ten
men needed in order to pray). My son told him he was unable to

come. He had cancer and felt quite ill. The shocked rabbi muttered some hasty words about prayer, hung up, and never called again. Because of his insensitivity, I did not ask him to officiate at the funeral but I did ask him to come to the house each evening during Shiva to say the customary prayers. He performed the prayer functions, insisted on adhering strictly to dogma, even though the family asked him to relax the requirements, and left without a private word to me, my husband, or our daughters. We never saw or heard from him again.

Felicia's experience with three different priests echoed the experience I had.

I was brought up devoutly Catholic. I believed since early childhood that if I prayed to God, He would hear me and answer my prayers. I really believed that if I prayed everything would be okay. I said my Hail Mary's in that little room in the hospital. I prayed like an idiot. I actually believed that.

Throughout my life, I prayed every night before I went to sleep to keep my family safe. I went to church every weekend. I did everything I was supposed to do, by the book.

Now I don't believe in any of that stuff anymore. I don't go to church anymore except for family functions. My sister switched religions. She became Lutheran. The church never taught us how to deal with this.

Amy's fourth birthday was one week after her death. The priest, who knew the family well, mentioned that at the funeral service, that her birthday was the following week. He said he'd stop by. He never called and never came. It was easier for him not to deal with me. How many other people in his parish had lost a four-year-old that he could just forget?

About two years later, my mother insisted that I speak with her priest. He made an appointment to see me. An hour after he was supposed to be at my house, I called him. He said he forgot but that he'd be right over. I told him to forget it.

A third priest who was close to the family sat down to talk

to me. He told me that two years was long enough for me to grieve and that I should be over it. I told him he didn't know what he was talking about. I wanted to hit him.

Felicia

I went to the priest in my parish; he mumbled something about prayer. I asked him how much education he had in bereavement and he said he had a course in the seminary. I walked out of there and never spoke to the clergy about my pain again.

Pauline

The priest came to the hospital but he wouldn't come inside my son's room because he had AIDS.

Anna

The clergy as clergy were of virtually no help to families in mourning. The clergy who became compassionate and caring friends were invaluable.

Belief in Reunion

John Bramblett echoed the sentiments of many of the parents we interviewed in the quote at the beginning of this chapter when he said, ". . . either this tragic world was all there was or there was something far greater beyond this life that I did not yet comprehend." Death as a finality is an impossible concept for a large number of bereaved parents. So many parents I interviewed spontaneously mentioned that they looked forward to reunion with their children in an afterlife that I began to ask parents who did not hit upon the subject spontaneously, "Do you expect to be reunited with your child?" The immediate and emphatic response often was, "Absolutely!" The response came from people of all faiths, from the devout to the nonobservant, from young and old. These parents *knew* their child was not gone, but existed in another plane, a different dimension. A few, whom we will discuss later in this chapter, consulted psychics in order to make contact with their child. The belief in an afterlife provides hope, allowing parents to go on with this life secure in the knowledge that the loss is not permanent.

I will listen to anyone who talks of a hereafter. I want to believe in reincarnation, that I will see Alison again, that this is not random but that there is some plan, that we will all be walking through a happy garden some day.

Shirley

It's a great relief to know that I will meet her in the next world. I feel that intensely.

Charles

I know exactly how he's going to greet me, with that great bear hug of his.

Sherry

I know my daughter is alive somewhere else and I'll see her again. I will see her smiling face.

Josie

I know Jess [recently deceased husband] is with Jaime. I don't know how people can live life without a belief in an afterlife. I always believed there's an afterlife and I know in my heart that Jaime and Jess are in a better state than here. I know Jaime is with his father.

Cass

When I see Douglas again, I'd like to know the form he'll be in. Will he still be three; or will he be thirty-three?

Denise

Even for those who are not certain of an afterlife, the idea remains compelling. Their child continues to exist in their consciousness as an inspiration.

I don't believe in an afterlife; but I do. I often have the feeling that Thomas is directing what I'm doing. I know what he would have wanted. His essence still exists. I know he'll be waiting for me.

Betty

I am not one of the lucky ones who believes in an afterlife. I don't have the consoling feeling that some day I will be able to give my son a hug again. I feel cheated compared to some of the parents I interviewed who derive a measure of peace from believing they will be reunited. But to me dead is dead; cold reality. I am writing this section in January, the month of Steven's birthday when I always go to the cemetery to visit his grave. I look down at the inscription I chose for his footstone. GONE SKIING. Talk about contradictions.

Psychic Phenomenon

My son asked me if I read anything that isn't about death. I read intensively about all kinds of religions, anybody that believes in an afterlife. I read the books about near-death experiences, about psychics, astrologers, reincarnation. I wasn't satisfied. There's this one psychic who has been on TV and someone in TCF told me about him and I went to see him. It's given me quite a sense of hope. Prior to Marion's death, I never thought about these things at all. Now I wonder how I will know Marion's voice when I see her again. I need so desperately to see her again. It just can't be that this is all there is. There's got to be more to life!!

Margot

Margot was one of several parents we interviewed who gravitated toward the paranormal, seeking contact with their children and affirmation of their continued existence.

I don't even doubt a life after death. Tanya could not just be gone. I have gone to see George Anderson, who has written several books on the subject of afterlife, *We Don't Die* and *Our Children Forever.* I had a wonderful reading with him. He was connecting with her. He knew about the scholarship we set up. He knew about her expressions and about how she died. He told me about the pink roses she gave me. There was no way he could have known that unless he was connecting with her. Tanya talks to him and he relays her messages to me.

Veronica

I went to a psychic to try to contact my daughter. I found the experience interesting and comforting.

Jill

How psychics know what they know is beyond our current knowledge. All that is clear from these interviews is that the parents who had readings with people who claim psychic powers came away eased and more peaceful.

Mystical Connections

Inspiration, mystical connection, signs, and symbols . . . Parents feel the enduring presence of their child in so many ways.

I had a visit from my son and he reassured me that heaven is the best place.

Regina

I finished Fordham University last year and I realized that it is the time that he would have finished. I think there is definitely an element of unconscious process. If I trust it, it will lead me in the right direction.

Donna

Regina faced an emotional crisis when she bought a new home and was about to move from the house she'd shared with her son. She needed to find some way to leave without feeling that she was abandoning a connection with the child whose memory lived within those walls.

> The day of the closing, when I did the final walk-through, I wanted to punch holes in the walls because I was so angry. I felt guilty about leaving Kevin behind, as if he were in the house and I was deserting him. I went into my bedroom and looked out the window at the window box and there was a whole slew of butterflies. [Butterflies are the symbol of TCF.] So I knew that Kevin said it was okay for me to move. That was his signal.

When Arlene's best friend died, she looked for a sign that her friend and her son were together. She saw an advertisement that mentioned places that were meaningful to both her friend and son and took that as the needed sign. Coincidence? Sign? Message from another dimension? Wrong questions. The only important reality lay in the fact that the sign had truth for Arlene and brought her repose.

Memorials

Connections are vital. Connections are maintained through memorials and traditions that parents establish to honor the memory of their child.

In Jewish tradition, it is customary for anyone who visits a gravesite to place a small stone on the headstone. Bruce began his own tradition of bringing home stones from each vacation to put on the headstone of Perry's grave. In that way, he stays connected and can bring home a memento for the child he lost.

Gloria is a collector of antiques.

> One of my dear friends gave me an oil lamp after Stuart's death that we light on every family occasion. I take it with me. On one occasion, I forgot it and my son-in-law came all the way back here and got it. It's a joy; the little ones know

what it is. There's a wonderful little book called *Freddy the Leaf* that explains death to little children. So the kids know about death. We just tell them that this lamp is in memory of Uncle Stuart. My oldest grandson asks to light it. They all like to light it.

Stuart remains a vital presence for each family member and for the children who never knew him. He is woven into the family history with this glowing reminder.

My sister set up Kevin's Corner at the children's library. Each year for his birthday, my family and friends donate books.

Regina

One family's memorial to their son started on impulse and grew into a local project that enriched their community. Betty's son, Tom, was killed in a skiing accident during Christmas week. The first Christmas after he died, Betty found herself browsing through a department store. She found a lovely sweater and immediately thought, "I have to buy that for Tom. He'd love it." Reality descended like a sledgehammer. Recovering her equilibrium, Betty decided to purchase the sweater she had been admiring. She proceeded to the next counter and bought several pairs of gloves and scarves and had all her purchases attractively gift wrapped. She took the packages home and put them in several shopping bags. Her husband, Trevor, was scheduled to go to New York City by bus the following day. She asked him to take her gifts and distribute them to any homeless people he encountered in the Port Authority Bus Terminal. He gladly did so.

Betty and Trevor were joined by their daughter-in-law, Tom's wife. They seized on the idea as a perfect memorial to Tom, who had been an avid advocate for the homeless. The three learned of a second-grade teacher in the local school who was doing a unit on homelessness and asked her if she would like to participate in their project. The teacher requested of each child in her class that they send any money they were considering spending on a gift for her as a contribution to a fund for the homeless. The children also decided to contribute money they would have spent for the classroom gifts they traditionally bought for one another. Some $125 was collected in the classroom and used to purchase warm clothing for the homeless. The family added these gifts to their own purchases. Soon, friends and extended family members joined the project. They decided, in later years, to give the gifts through shelters for the homeless and went on the anniversary of Tom's death to distribute the donations. They spoke with the homeless people to learn more about their plight. Trevor went to the second-grade classroom to tell the children about the lives of the people to whom he gave their gifts.

The tradition has continued through the decade since Tom's accident. Each year the family collects donations and spends the anniversary of Tom's death bringing warm clothing and warm wishes to the homeless.

Memorials are a living tribute and loving reminder of the child's life. Here are some of the ways in which parents continue to keep the memory of their child green:

- Sherry and Matt gave an article of their son's clothing to each of the other children in the family. Sherry says she especially likes to wear his jackets.
- Josie and her family go out to dinner together each year to celebrate Ginny's birthday. Even these many years later, the older children, now grown, still come home for the occasion.
- Denise's friends and neighbors planted a tree at the local library. Like Josie's family, Denise marks her son's birthday by going on a special outing, doing something that her son would have enjoyed.
- Tom planted a memorial garden.
- Karen compiled her daughter's poetry into a book. She said some of those poems were read at her son's wedding.
- Betty collected her son's writings into a book she is trying to have published.
- Keith goes to the pediatrics ward of the local hospital to play Santa Claus each Christmas in memory of his son.

Numerous families made and continue to make charitable donations.

- Gretchen's yearly yard sale has become a community institution. People from all over the neighborhood bring their salable items for the event. The proceeds are donated for research into cystic fibrosis.
- Pauline donated a computer room to her son's high school.
- Margot, Harold, and Anne each established awards for academic excellence in their child's name.
- Veronica and Alan each established scholarship funds. Both keep in touch with the recipients.
- Charles and Barbara established a foundation to purchase laboratory equipment and make donations to the Ronald McDonald House. They developed a group of blood donors for the local hospital.
- Each year on the anniversary of Sid's death, his family sends donations to the Make-a-Wish Foundation.

Parents not only give monetary donations, many also donate their time generously.

- Donna, Theda, and Gretchen each started bereavement groups in their community.
- Joanne does volunteer work with battered women and with babies who have AIDS.
- Regina, Cass, Margot, Alan, Pauline, Veronica, Rhoda, Barry, Thomas, Stephanie, Loretta, and Min each remain in leadership capacities in The Compassionate Friends many years later. They organize meetings, write the newsletters, and talk at length on the phone to the newly bereaved whenever they are needed.

The manner of death leads many parents to address societal ills. Mothers Against Drunk Driving, as mentioned earlier, is the activist group that was begun by the mother of a girl who was killed by a drunk driver. The conscience of a nation has been raised and laws enacted as a result of the work of these bereaved parents and their supporters.

- Sherry is active in lobbying for gun control. She also became an advocate for the promotion of a "Bill of Rights for Crime Victims" to ensure that families know they are entitled to have funeral expenses reimbursed, that victims are entitled to some financial compensation, and that they are entitled to have the fees for counseling reimbursed by a Victim Compensation Fund.
- Theda became a social worker and has devoted two decades to counseling survivors after suicide and families of murder victims.
- Rachel is active in promoting drug awareness programs in local high schools.

Visiting the cemetery and caring for the grave, reminiscing, keeping items of special significance for the child are additional ways parents remain in touch. There wasn't a home I entered that did not have pictures of the child they lost displayed prominently. Those pictures are treasured and keep the memory alive.

A number of parents write. Patrice continues after fourteen years to write poems to Sid whenever she is so moved. The following is the poem she wrote on the day he would have graduated from high school.

> This should be a time of promise . . .
> A time for fun . . .
> This would have been your high school graduation.
> There should be laughter, pride, and joy . . .
> But not for me, not for my boy.
> Instead there are tears and a great deal of pain.
> It's a time we reflect on what could have been.
> In a few short weeks you would have been eighteen . . .
> So many hopes . . . So many dreams . . .
> None of which will ever be seen.
> One would think that after fourteen years,

There wouldn't be so much pain . . .
There wouldn't be any more tears.
And still after all these years,
It breaks my heart that I will never see . . .
My son in cap and gown . . .
Celebrating with the class of '93.

Each of these memorials represents a family's tribute to their child. Each represents a way in which the family brings meaning back into lives that were stripped of purpose. Each speaks to the truth that there is comfort and healing in generosity.

One of the supreme acts of generosity comes from the broken-hearted parents who found the compassion to open their hearts and donate their child's organs for transplant. These many years later, each parent confirmed that this was a good decision, one they have never regretted, one that has given them the consolation of knowing that they did what was right and good.

If anything is to be learned from the journeys of these many families, it is a lesson of hope. The lesson teaches that we rebound slowly, over many years and decades. Unlike the river whose course always seeks the lowest level, the human spirit seems consistently to seek a higher plain. We find that meaning and purpose have evolved out of the chaos of our devastation.

If I can come to any generalizations, I would say that I saw strength of character emerge. I saw what I can only call a more mature sense of values. We have reordered our priorities and put in perspective what is really important to us in life. We hold more tightly to our loved ones and give more generously of ourselves. Having known pain, we are more attuned to it in others. We have gained confidence from knowing that we have survived hell. Having dwelled in the darkness, we appreciate the light. Living with the sadness that is always background music, the strains of a beautiful melody now sound all the more poignant. We have learned humility, to take what life has to offer and to make of it the very best we can. We know that we can never trust what is ahead but that we have the courage to face whatever it may be.

THRESHOLD

Every year I am shocked by spring.
Here it comes suddenly, like a curtain
made of colorful print material, dropping,
transforming the land.

Each year
I feel like I haven't been paying attention.
One morning I wake and my world is gaudy with color,
giddy—like someone shook the champagne
and it spilled, its effervescence
waking the flowers early, drunk and in love.

There is no memory of the neon leaves of fall.
Winter's wind has pushed on.
I'm glad it's gone.
It had become a guest who stayed too long
a bore that drove me to my room.

Each year when the azaleas bloom,
I remember another spring.
That one wore a pall.
The rain would not stop. It poured
into the open grave of my son.
It poured deep into my heart.
I was sure it would never,
ever,
stop.

It did,
though I sometimes wished it hadn't.
I was stuck between forgetting
and remembering.
Remembering won.
Now I see his face in the azaleas.
They bloomed that spring while he died.

I no longer hold it against them.

—Fay Harden

Further Reading for Parents and Caregivers

Arnold, Joan Hagen, and Penelope Bushman Gemma. 1994. *A child dies: A portrait of family grief.* Rockville, Md.: Aspen Systems Corporation.

Blankenship, Jayne. 1984. *In the center of the night: Journey through a bereavement.* New York: Putnam.

Bolton, Iris. 1983. *My son . . . my son . . . A guide to healing after a suicide in the family.* Belmore Way, Ga.: Bolton Press.

Bordow, Joan. 1982. *The ultimate loss—Coping with the death of a child.* New York: Beaufort Books.

Bramblett, John. 1991. *When good-bye is forever: Learning to live again after the loss of a child.* New York: Ballantine Books.

Davis, Deborah. 1991. *Empty cradle, broken heart: Surviving the death of your baby.* Golden, Colo.: Fulcrum.

Donnelly, Katherine Fair. 1982. *Recovering from the loss of a child.* New York: Macmillan.

Edelstein, Linda. 1984. *Maternal bereavement: Coping with the unexpected death of a child.* New York: Praeger.

Finkbeiner, Ann. 1996. *After the death of a child: Living with the loss through the years.* New York: Free Press.

Heavilin, Marilyn W. 1993. *Roses in December: Finding strength within grief.* Nashville, Tenn.: Thomas Nelson.

Klass, Dennis. 1988. *Parental grief: Solace and resolution.* New York: Springer.

Knapp, Ronald J. 1986. *Beyond endurance: When a child dies.* New York: Schocken Books.

Kushner, Harold. 1987. *When bad things happen to good people.* New York: Random House.

Lightner, Candy and Nancy Hathaway. 1990. *Giving sorrow words.* New York: Warner Books.

Parkes, Colin M. and Robert S. Weiss. 1983. *Recovery from bereavement.* New York: Basic Books.

Rando, Therese A. 1988. *Grieving: How to go on living when someone you love dies.* Lexington, Mass.: Lexington Books.

———— ed. 1986. *Parental loss of a child.* Champaign, Ill.: Research Press.

Raphael, Beverly. 1983. *The anatomy of bereavement.* New York: Basic Books.

Rosen, Helen. 1986. *Unspoken grief: Coping with childhood sibling loss.* Lexington, Mass.: Lexington Books.

Rosof, Barbara D. 1994. *The worst loss: How families heal from the death of a child.* New York: Henry Holt.

Sanders, Catherine M. 1992. *Surviving grief and learning to live again.* New York: John Wiley.

———— 1992. *How to survive the loss of a child: Filling the emptiness and rebuilding your life.* Rocklin, Cal.: Prima.

Schiff, Harriet S. 1977. *The bereaved parent.* New York: Crown.

Solin, Ann and John Guinan. 1993. *Healing after the suicide of a loved one.* New York: Fireside/Simon & Schuster.

Tatelbaum, Judy. 1980. *The courage to grieve.* New York: Lippincott and Crowell.

Toder, Francine. 1986. *When your child is gone.* Sacramento, Cal.: Capital.

Wolterstorff, Nicholas. 1987. *Lament for a son.* Grand Rapids, Mich.: Eerdmans.

References for Professionals

Bernstein, Paula P., S. Wayne Duncan, Leslie A. Gavin, Kristen M. Lindahl, and Sally Ozonoff. 1989. Resistance to psychotherapy after a child dies: The effects of death on parents and siblings. *Psychotherapy,* 26, 227–32.

Binger, C. M., A. R. Ablin, R. C. Feuerstein, J. H. Kushner, S. Zoger, and C. Mikkelsen. 1969. Childhood leukemia: Emotional impact on patient and family. *The New England Journal of Medicine,* Feb. 20, 414–19.

Bohannon, Judy R. 1991. Religiosity related to grief levels of bereaved mothers and fathers. *Omega,* Vol. 23(2), 153–59.

Braun, Mildred J., and Dale H. Berg. 1994. Meaning reconstruction in the experience of parental bereavement. *Death Studies,* 18:105–29.

Cain, A. and B. Cain. 1964. On replacing a child. *Journal of the American Academy of Child Psychiatrists,* 3, 443–56.

Cook, Judith A. 1983. A death in the family: Parental bereavement in the first year. *Suicide and Life-threatening Behavior,* Vol. 13(1), 42–61.

———— 1988. Dad's double binds: Rethinking fathers' bereavement from a men's studies perspective. *Journal of Contemporary Ethnography,* Vol.17, No.3, 285–308.

Davies, Betty, John Spinetta, Ida Martinson, Sandra McClowry, and Emily Kulenkamp. 1986. Manifestations of levels of functioning in grieving families. *Journal of Family Issues,* Vol. 7, No.3, 297–313.

Flesch, Regina. 1975. A guide to interviewing the bereaved. *Journal of Thanatology,* Vol. 3:93–103.

Frankl, Victor E. 1959. *Man's search for meaning.* Boston: Beacon.

Gelcer, Esther. 1983. Mourning is a family affair. *Family Process,* 22, 501–16.

Hare-Mustin, Rachel T. 1979. Family therapy following the death of a child. *Journal of Marital and Family Therapy,* April, 51–59.

Hellmrath, Thomas A., and Elaine M. Steinitz. 1978. Parental grieving and the failure of social support. *Journal of Family Practice,* 6:785–89.

Kallenberg, Kjell, and Bjorn Soderfeldt. 1992. Three years later: Grief, view of life, and personal crisis after death of a family member. *Journal of Palliative Care,* 8:4, 13–19.

Kerner, John, Birt Harvey, and Norman Lewiston. 1979. The impact of grief: A retrospective study of family function following the loss of a child with cystic fibrosis. *Journal of Chronic Disease,* 32:221–25.

Klass, Dennis. 1986-7. Marriage and divorce among bereaved parents in a self-help group. *Omega,* Vol. 17(3) 237–49.

Klerman, Gerald L., and Judith E. Izen. 1977. The effects of bereavement and grief on physical health and general well being. *Advances in Psychosomatic Medicine,* 9:63–104.

Koocher, Gerald. 1994. Preventive intervention following a child's death. *Psychotherapy,* Vol. 31, No. 3, 377–82.

Krell, Robert, and Leslie Rabkin. 1979. The effects of sibling death on the surviving child: A family perspective. *Family Process,* Vol. 18, 471–77.

Kubler-Ross, Elisabeth. 1969. *On death and dying.* New York: Macmillan.

Lehman, Darrin R., Camille B. Wortman, and Allan F. Williams. 1987. Long-term effects of losing a spouse or child in a motor vehicle crash. *Journal of Personality and Social Psychology,* Vol. 52, No. 1, 218–31

Levy, Leon H., and Joyce F. Derby. 1992. Bereavement support groups: Who joins, who does not, and why. *American Journal of Community Psychology,* Vol. 20, No.5, 649–62.

Levy, Leon H., Joyce F. Derby, and Karen S. Martinkowski. 1992. The question of who participates in bereavement research and the bereavement risk index. *Omega,* Vol. 25(3),225–38.

Lundin, Tom. 1984. Morbidity following sudden and unexpected bereavement. *British Journal of Psychiatry*, 144, 84–88.

Martinson, Ida M., Betty Davies, and Sandra McClowry. 1991. Parental depression following the death of a child. *Death Studies,* 15:259–67.

Martinson, Ida M., and Rosemary Campos. 1991. Adolescent bereavement: long-term responses to a sibling's death from cancer. *Journal of Adolescent Research,* Vol. 6, No.1, 54–69.

McClowry, S.G., E. B. Davies, K. A. May, E. J. Kulenkamp, and I. M. Martinson. 1987. The empty space phenomenon: The process of grief in the bereaved family. *Death Studies*, 11, 361–74.

McCown, Darlene E., and Clara Pratt. 1985. Impact of sibling death on children's behavior. *Death Studies*, 9:323–35.

McKeever, Patricia. 1983. Siblings of chronically ill children: A literature review with implications for research and practice. *American Journal of Orthopsychiatry,* 53(2), 209–17.

Miles, Margaret S., and Alice S. Demi. 1983–4. Toward the development of a theory of bereavement guilt: Sources of guilt in bereaved parents. *Omega,* Vol. 4(4), 299–314.

Moore, Ida M., Catherine L. Gillis, and Ida M. Martinson. 1988. Psychosomatic symptoms in parents 2 years after the death of a child with cancer. *Nursing Research,* Vol. 37, No. 2, March/April.

Ness, David E., and Cynthia R. Pfeffer. 1990. Sequelae of bereavement resulting from suicide. *American Journal of Psychiatry*, 147:3, 279–85, March.

Owen, Greg, Robert Fulton, and Eric Markusen. 1982–3. Death at a distance: A study of family survivors. *Omega*, Vol. 13 (3) 191–224.

Parkes, C. Murray, Ira O. Glick, Robert S. Weiss. 1974. *The first year of bereavement*. New York: John Wiley and Sons.

Pollock, George. 1986. Childhood sibling loss: A family tragedy. *Psychiatric Annals*, 16:5, 309–14.

Ponzetti, James, and Mary Johnson. 1991. The forgotten grievers: Grandparents' reactions to the death of grandchildren. *Death Studies*, 15:157–67.

Ponzetti, James. 1992. Bereaved families: A comparison of parents' and grandparents' reactions to the death of a child. *Omega*, Vol. 25(1), 63–71.

Poznandki, E. O. 1972. The replacement child: An unresolved saga of parental grief. *Behavioral Pediatrics*, 81:1190–93.

Rando, Therese A. 1983. An investigation of grief and adaptation in parents whose child died from cancer. *Journal of Pediatric Psychology*, Vol. 8, No. 1, 3–20.

————— 1985. Bereaved parents: Particular difficulties, unique factors, and treatment issues. *Social Work*, 30, 19–23.

————— 1986. *Loss and anticipatory grief*. Lexington, Mass: Lexington Books.

Range, Lillian M., and Nathan M. Niss. 1990. Long-term bereavement from suicide, homicide, accidents, and natural deaths. *Death Studies*, 14:423–33.

Raphael, Beverly, and Warwick Middleton. 1990. What is pathologic grief? *Psychiatric Annals*, Vol. 20, No. 6, 304–07.

Raphael, Beverly, and David C. Maddison. 1976. The care of bereaved adults. *Modern Trends in Psychosomatic Medicine*, ed. O. W. Hill, London: Butterworth.

Rosen, Elliott J. 1988–9. Family therapy in cases of interminable grief for the loss of a child. *Omega*, Vol. 19 (3), 187–201.

Rosenblatt, Paul, Linda H. Burns. 1986. Long-term effects of perinatal loss. *Journal of Family Issues*, 7, 237–53.

Rubin, Simon. 1981. A two-track model of bereavement: Theory and application in research. *American Journal of Orthopsychhiatry*, 51 (1), 101–9, January.

——— 1989–90. Death of the future?: An outcome study of bereaved parents in Israel. *Omega*, Vol. 20(4), 323–39.

——— 1991–2. Adult child loss and the two-track model of bereavement. *Omega*, Vol. 24(3), 183–202.

Rudestam, Kjell Erik. 1977. Physical and psychological responses to suicide in the family. *Journal of Consulting and Clinical Psychology*, Vol. 45, No. 2, 162–70.

Rynearson, Edward. 1990. Pathologic bereavement. *Psychiatric Annals*, Vol. 20, No. 6, 295–344.

Sanders, Catherine M. 1988. Risk factors in bereavement outcome. *Journal of Social Issues*, Vol. 44, No. 3, 97–111.

——— 1980. A comparison of adult bereavement in the death of a spouse, child, and parent. *Omega*, Vol. 10(4), 303–21.

——— 1989. *Grief: The mourning after*. New York: John Wiley and Sons.

Schoenberg, Bernard, Irwin Gerber, Alfred Wiener, Austin Kutscher, David Peretz, and Arthur Carr. 1975. *Bereavement: Its psychosocial aspects*. New York: Columbia University Press.

Schulz, Richard. 1978. *The psychology of death, dying, and bereavement*. Massachusetts: Addison-Wesley.

Schwab, Reiko. 1990. Paternal and maternal coping with the death of a child. *Death Studies*, 14: 407–22.

———— 1992. Effects of a child's death on the marital relationship: A preliminary study. *Death Studies*, 16:141–54.

Shanfield, Stephen B., and Barbara J. Swain. 1984. Death of adult children in traffic accidents. *Journal of Nervous and Mental Disease*, Vol. 172, No. 9, 533–38.

Shanfield, Stephen B., G. Andrew H. Benjamin, and Barbara J. Swain. 1984. Parents' reactions to the death of an adult child from cancer. *American Journal of Psychiatry*, 141:9, 1092–94.

Sheskin, Arlene, and Samuel Wallace. 1976. Differing bereavements: Suicide, natural, and accidental death. *Omega*, Vol. 7(3), 229–41.

Soricelli, Barbara, and Carolyn L. Utech. 1985. Mourning the death of a child: The family and group process. *Social Work*, 30, 429–34.

Spinetta, John J., Joyce Swarner, and John P. Sheposh. 1981. Effective parental coping following the death of a child from cancer. *Journal of Pediatric Psychology*, Vol. 6, 151–63.

Tooley, K. 1975. The choice of a surviving sibling as the "scapegoat" in some cases of maternal bereavement: A case report. *The Journal of Child Psychology and Psychiatry*, 16:331–39.

Videka-Sherman, Lynn. 1982. Coping with the death of a child: A study over time. *American Journal of Orthopsychiatry*, 52(4):688–98.

Volkan, Vamik, and Elizabeth Zintl. 1993. *Life after loss*. New York: Charles Scribner's Sons.

Whitis, P. R. 1968. The legacy of a child's suicide. *Family Process*, 7(2):159–68.

Wortman, Camille B., and Roxane C. Silver. 1989. The myths of coping with loss. *Journal of Consulting and Clinical Psychology*, Vol. 57, No. 3, 349–57.

Photo by Michael Janis

Judith R. Bernstein, Ph.D., is a psychologist practicing in New Jersey. Since the death of her son in 1987, she has combined her personal and professional knowledge to help guide other parents along the painful journey after the loss of a child. She has counseled, written, lectured, and been interviewed by the media on the subject of parental bereavement. She is married to her tennis partner and dive buddy. She has two daughters, two sons-in-law, and three grandchildren.